BIG BIM little bim

The practical approach to building information modeling
Integrated Practice done the right way!

Finith E. Jernigan, AIA

First Edition

4Site Press
Salisbury, MD

Foreword

BIM transformed my business. It put me in the business of information in the Information Age and made me a better architect.

Whether you are an architect or engineer, an owner, an educator, a student or a builder, *BIG BIM little bim* will show you how to use technology to do a better job with less. It will show you time-tested and field-proven ways to make our world a better place.

The world of integrated architectural practice using Building Information Modeling (BIM) is expanding fast, almost too fast. Many are under pressure to adopt BIM, usually without much planning. The decision always comes with a big software purchase attached. The challenges seem formidable.

BIM is not new. Some firms have used BIM for nearly two decades. BIM gives you more time to do the things you like to do and automates the mundane. *BIG BIM little bim* will help you to understand how to achieve this balance.

The change becomes less intimidating when you realize that you already have many of the answers. The process is very similar to what you have been doing for years. This book will help you understand how to adjust and integrate BIM successfully into your practice. Making the migration increases your relevancy and value. It will help you have an immediate impact on your business.

Most are already familiar with *little bim*. Few are familiar with *BIG BIM*. With *little bim* you do what you have always done, only better. *BIG BIM* takes you many steps beyond. This book explains the difference.

The "I" in BIM is information. That is where the opportunities exist. That is where the value is. *BIG BIM* promotes real sustainability. It connects the dots, improves information flow, and supports integration. It interacts with the world we inhabit. By assembling knowledge and integrating a long view of our environment, BIG BIM moves you beyond bamboo floors. There are immediate benefits for any organization.

No single software product or *little bim* process offers a magic BIM button; the construction industry is too complex. Together *BIG BIM* and *little bim* let you find the opportunities in this complexity. You become more relevant and more valuable as you move into this new world. The challenges are familiar. The tools and processes exist to support the challenge. It's up to you.

Kimon G. Onuma, AIA

*President of Onuma Architects and
BIM user since 1993.
2007 Winner of the AIA BIM and,
FIATECH CETI awards.*

What's in it for me?

Be productive. Keep food on the table and the kids in college. Become more successful. Keep your clients happy.

Integrated practice offers the best way to do any or all of these. This book is not about which software product is best for you. It is not about buying a new computer system. This book is about the ins and outs of changing your business to take advantage of technology and make it work for you.

If you are starting out...

You are a junior staff member, a student or, about to start your first firm.

This book will provide context and an overview. It will help you to tell others about integration. It will help in your personal exploration. It will explain how to structure your new business to be a leader in building sustainable value within the complex network that makes up the built environment.

If you are a facility user or owner...

This book will be an eye-opener. It makes a case, which, for you, may seem obvious. You will wonder why not all architects have been doing this all along. It will give you ideas for changes to your organization that let you benefit from the process.

If you are a small established firm...

This book will give you the resources to identify changes that move you toward an integrated practice.

Take it one-step at a time. It will help you become more effective and more profitable.

If you are a medium established firm...

This book will give you a framework for developing your firm's business case for change. It will help you to move beyond a focus on buying new applications. It will give you a plan for keeping the parts of your business that work and replacing those that do not provide sustainable value to your clients.

If you are a large established firm...

This book will support your business case for integrated practice. You will recognize this book as a roadmap for your organizational change management process.

If you are a builder or contractor...

This book will show you that some architects "get it." You have been hearing rumblings about virtual design and construction through your professional organizations. You may have heard about some of the construction success stories. This book will give you an overview of what architects are up to, and it will start you thinking about how the process can make you more money and keep your clients happier.

If you are an engineer...

This book will give you an overview of why owners and your architect clients think that BIM is necessary. It will give you a better understanding of the forces that are driving this need. It will help you to understand how important it is that you also make this change.

BIG BIM little bim

The practical approach to building information modeling
Integrated Practice done the right way!

4Site Press

130 East Main Street
Salisbury, MD 21801-5038, USA
fulfillment@4sitesystems.com
http://www.4sitesystems.com

Unattributed quotations are by Finith Jernigan.

Jernigan, Finith E.
    Big BIM little BIM : the practical approach to building information model-ing : integrated practice done the right way! / [Finith E. Jernigan]. -- 1st ed.
    p. cm.
    Includes bibliographical references.
    LCCN 2007903839
    ISBN-13: 978-0-9795699-0-6
    ISBN-10: 0-9795699-0-7

    1. Building--Data processing. 2. Building management--Data processing.
    3. Communication in the building trades. 4. Architectural practice.
    5. Architects and builders.   I. Title. II. Title: Practical approach to building information modeling.

    TH437.J47 2007   690.0285   QBI07-600254

Publisher: 4Site Press, Salisbury, Maryland

Printed in the United States

Warning and Disclaimer

We designed this book to be a guide for information modeling and integrated practice. It is sold with the understanding that the publisher and author are not engaged in rendering legal, insurance, or accounting services. If you require legal or other expert assistance, you should seek the services of a competent professional.

This book does not reprint all the information that is available to those transitioning to building information modeling. Instead, it complements, amplifies, and supplements other texts. We urge you to read all the available material, learn as much as possible about integrated practice and BIM, and tailor the information to your individual requirements. For more information, see the many resources in the Appendix.

We have made every effort to make this book as complete and accurate as possible. However, there may be mistakes, both typographical and in content. Furthermore, this book contains information on BIM and integrated practice that is current up to the publishing date. The purpose of this book is to educate and entertain. Quotations used in this book remain the intellectual property of their originators. We do not assert any claim of copyright for individual quotations. By quoting authors, we do not in any way mean to imply their endorsement or approval of our concepts. To the best of our knowledge, all quotes included here fall under the fair use or public domain guidelines of copyright law in the United States. The author and 4Site Press shall have neither liability nor responsibility to any person or entity with respect to any loss or damage caused, or alleged to have been caused, directly or indirectly, by the information contained in this book.

If you do not wish to be bound by the above, you may return this book for a full refund.

Acknowledgements

This book is a memorial to Paul Kratzer. Everyone should have a friend like Paul Kratzer once in his or her life. Paul's zany style and out-of-the-box approach to marketing and life inspired us all. His push to simplify BIM so that it could be "sold like soap" helped us to simplify our message.

I have not attempted to cite all the authorities and sources consulted in preparation of this book. To do so would require more space than is available. The list would include federal government agencies, AIA chapters, clients, libraries, institutions, and many individuals. I would like to acknowledge the following individuals for their special contributions; without their input, advice, and feedback, this book would have never happened:

Special thanks to W. Frank Brady, the world's first 4SiteManager. Without Frank keeping his head in the game and getting the work out the door, I would never have had the time to work on this book.

Hal Adkins, director of Public Works, and Terry McGean, PE, city engineer for the Town of Ocean City, MD; William Gordy, deputy fire chief, Salisbury, MD; and Sue Simmons, director of Recreation and Parks, Caroline County, MD. They were the first clients to "get it." Without good clients, none of this would be possible.

Douglas Aldinger, PE, of Erdman Anthony Engineering in Harrisburg, PA; Paul Adams, AIA, of Earth and Sky Architects in Denver; David Wigodner, AIA, of Interwork Architecture in Northbrook, IL; Ginie Lynch in Salisbury, MD; and Jack K. Rogers, AIA, in Dagsboro, DE, all provided editorial input and feedback.

Hugh Livingston, president of I.D.E.A.S., Inc. in Salisbury, MD; Heikki Kulusjarvi, president of Solibri Inc., in Helsinki; Dianne Davis, president of AEC Infosystems Inc., in Baltimore and Nina McKenzie, AIA, of Arch Street Software in San Diego, for their advice and systems that have made data work for us from the beginning. Without Chip Veise and Nelson Young of SPN Construction Managers in Rockville, MD, I probably would not "get it."

Without Chester Ross, I would never have learned that you do not ever have to grow old. It is a state of mind.

My thanks to Mike Lokey for his consistent advice and understanding, Fay Smack for her long and steady friendship and hard work and, my parents Finith and Vanita Jernigan for their advice and encouragement.

Special thanks to my sons Finith III and Devin. They have put up with BIM since before they were born.

Moreover, my most special thanks and all my love to Beth. Without her support, none of this would be possible.

Contributors

Much of the *Integrated Future* chapter was contributed by Kevin Connolly, AIA, of Milwaukee. Mr. Connolly is president of Connolly Architects and founder of the Triglyph Architectural Organization. Triglyph was one of the first collaborative groups designed to leverage architects' abilities within the BIM environment.

Much of the *Decision support systems* chapter was contributed by Kimon Onuma, AIA, president of Onuma Inc. of Pasadena. Mr. Onuma is a thought leader in the BIM world. His conception of the Object Genome, organizing the objects that underpin BIM technology, has helped many understand the complexity and power of the process. Mr. Onuma won the 2007 American Institute of Architects BIM award for the *US Coast Guard Web-Enabled BIM Projects* and the 2007 FIATECH CETI award for the *Sector Command Planning System for the US Coast Guard*. Design Atlantic Ltd worked on both projects with Onuma.

James Hyslop, president of Standing Stone Consulting Inc., of Huntingdon, PA, contributed much of the *Scenario based planning* chapter. Standing Stone specializes in Crime Prevention Through Environmental Design (CPTED), safety and security. With Onuma they created BIMBombs.

Table of Contents

PART I

ARE YOU READY TO CHANGE?

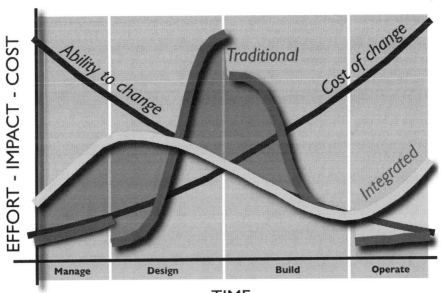

CHAPTER 1

Conceive the future

 Technology, coupled with owner demands for better, faster, less-costly projects and processes that are more effective, is driving change in the design and construction industry. *Integrated practice* is the term the American Institute of Architects is using to describe this new way of working.

At the core of an integrated architectural practice are teams composed of all project stakeholders, guided by principles of true collaboration, open information sharing, shared risks and rewards, just-in-time decision-making, and the use of the latest technology. With integrated practice, architects' design process is improved and they expand their value throughout the entire facility life cycle.

Let's face it, BIM needs to be put into context. The problem for most architects is that they make too many decisions at the wrong time, with too little information. Integrating technology does not require that architects throw away all of their proven tools and experiences. It does however require them to look at things differently. It requires them to separate the things that should be kept from those that should be replaced.

With integrated practice, architects become better designers.

Making the transition to integrated practice requires good planning. The change affects all aspects of how an architect does business. Done correctly, integrated practice changes how everyone looks at our world.

This book tells you how to do it right. It will help you to plan for the change. It will show you the right steps to take. It will show you the best way to avoid trouble. Like any good guide, it will tell you the best places to use your resources and the areas to avoid. You have to decide how fast you will make the change.

People accept change at different rates. Some prepare better. Some have more money, more support, and can handle faster transitions. Some like to go fast. Some like it slow and steady. You can tailor your process to your ability to handle change. We designed this book to give you direction, no matter how fast you proceed.

Integrate BIM

The acronym BIM (Building Information Modeling) was coined in early 2002 to describe virtual design, construction, and facilities management. BIM processes revolve around virtual models that make it possible to share information throughout the entire building industry. These virtual models are embedded with data which, when shared among design team members, greatly reduces errors and improves facilities. BIM offers owners the ability to become more efficient and effective by linking their business processes with their facilities. The federal government has predicted savings of over \$15.8 billion annually from integrated processes. Projects today save 5-12% when BIM is properly used.

This book will show you how to use BIM properly.

Building Information Modeling, coupled with Geographic information Systems (GiS), relational databases, and the Internet all help us to achieve Toffler's vision.

Building on these concepts, you can now use rules-based planning systems to capture and integrate knowledge at all levels. If you can describe something, it can be captured. If it can be captured, you can define its relationship to other knowledge. By applying the rules that govern how these bits of knowledge interact, you can assess options more quickly and more accurately than ever before. Where planning once relied on broad generalities and "rules of thumb," you can now simulate "real life" using BIM.

> Describing a "strategy of social futurism," Alvin Toffler, author of *Future Shock*, wrote that the capture of integrated knowledge in an organized way should drive planning. He wrote, "Attempts to bring this knowledge together would constitute one of the crowning intellectual efforts in history—and one of the most worthwhile."

Knowledge is an impermanent commodity. Technology has changed the world. Technology has even changed how we react to the world. We all have to become more adaptable and capable. We must process information faster. The issue is to decide how we will adapt to the changes.

Most people know that we have to adapt faster. We have seen how change has accelerated everything in the industry. Five years once seemed like a long time. Now five years happens in a relative instant. To manage change at this pace, decision-making must be better.

Today, architects, builders and owners are making too many errors by being conservative. Forecasts must have greater accuracy. We must become more flexible and must plan with longer horizons. Otherwise, improvement is not possible.

Clutching to the old ways is no longer the best solution. Technology gives us the opportunity to forecast with better data. It frees us to react quickly. It allows us to study change with detail. It provides the data to justify new design ideas.

We should all realize that it is better to "err on the side of daring"—because we are making too many cumulative mistakes and wasting resources using cautious approaches.

BIM done right

Throughout this book, you will see the term BIM used often. The term is confusing. BIM has no context for most people. Some see BIM as the modeling tools sold by vendors. Limiting yourself to a descriptive term for products sold by software companies diminishes the power and benefits you receive from BIM.

BIM is not a software application. BIM is an information-based system that builds long-term value and advances innovation. It improves how projects get designed and built. It builds economic value in many areas. It improves the environment and people's lives. We will study the reasons for this in later sections.

BIM is an evolutionary change in how people relate to the built environment. The speed of this change creates many opportunities for ambiguity. In this book, we define BIM as Beyond Information Models to align with the universal nature of the concept.

Conventions

For the purpose of clarity, we use the following conventions throughout this book:

bim (lower case) is used to represent applications-focused topics; i.e., ArchiCad, Bentley, and Revit are bim tools.

BIM (upper case) is the management of information and the complex relationships between the social and technical resources that represent the complexity, collaboration, and interrelationships of today's organizations and environment. The focus is on managing projects to get the right information to the right place at the right time.

Throughout this book, you will find references to the word "control." Control is another term that can be very ambiguous. It can be good or it can be bad, i.e., control as in "cracking the whip" or "control freak' is considered bad while control, as in "steering the boat" is considered good. In this book, "control" is about steering and guiding the process.

This book is an introduction to successful integrated practice in architecture. It focuses on actions, systems, and tools that you can use now. BIM/bim is such a wide-reaching process that, of necessity, we have not attempted to cover every option and all the available or emerging tools and systems. Today, there are literally too many to consider. Tomorrow there will be many more. Create your strategy to adapt the best of them as they emerge. Focus on those that you can use profitably today. By using the concepts in this book, you can do it right, adapting and growing as the technology continues to advance.

CHAPTER 2

Know where BIM leads

DREAMS ARE GOOD. WE ALL need dreams. When we quit dreaming, we stagnate. We lock into doing things the same way, repeatedly. Even when we do not get the results that, we (and our clients) want and expect.

Have you ever dreamed about a time when you could call up the site details for a new project—in real time? Without hiring a surveyor? Without visiting the site? Have you ever dreamed about a time when you could open a file and have all the as-built and as-operated details for the remodeling project that you just won? Have you ever wished that you could really understand how your new client's company works, without doing weeks of diagnostics and fact-finding? Well, now you can.

Building Information Modeling is, as a concept, so universal and so wide reaching that it can (and probably does) include nearly anything that you can think of. If it touches on the built environment, BIM processes can make it better and more efficient. This complexity has led many of the pioneers to be bogged down in an endless loop of adding detail upon detail. They have a lofty goal—to develop fully functional and user-friendly systems that everyone in the building world can use to interact with each other. They work to capture all of the information that our world revolves around. You cannot wait for them to finish.

If you do, you will be left behind.

You can have the benefits from BIM today. The tools are available—and have been for twenty years. That is why we talk about *Simple BIM.*

- Simple BIM is about getting results, using BIM—right now.

- Simple BIM lets you use the tools and processes that work well—right now.

- Simple BIM lets you make sure that you position yourself to take advantage of other technologies as they become commercially available.

You and your clients cannot wait for someone else to figure out all of the complex systems and standards for you. You have within your current resources and available tools, the ability to deliver many of the benefits of BIM, today. Moreover, using these resources and tools in new ways, you have the ability to produce better architecture and happier clients.

Why not get started?

Sometimes, you have to overcome many issues before you can change. There is a lot of inertia to overcome. However, if you look at BIM as a business decision to deliver better design and better client support, it becomes simple.

A client's struggle

"Design is the honeymoon period. I manage facilities for a 400-bed medical center and we are always under construction. We hire architects and they create wonderful concepts—everybody loves the concepts.

If we have hired a construction manager to control the design process, we get solid information. If not, we look to the architect for details to assure ourselves that the design meets all of our needs. We get 'pretty pictures', but we rarely get dependable decision-making information from the architect at this stage. The images excite our staff. The architect asks us to take it on faith that everything is worked out. The decision to move forward becomes strongly weighted by emotion rather than by facts.

By the time we are able to understand the details, the architect has invested a lot of time developing the design. If everything is on track, life is good. If not, someone spends a lot of money to make corrections. Unfortunately, the costs often fall on us since we approved the 'pretty pictures'. The tendency is to proceed after tweaking the concept, since no one wants to spend the money or take the time to start over.

When we receive bids in this environment, they are often drastically over budget. Then everyone panics and the architect gets defensive. The project gets "bought out" or "value engineered" and things get lost in the process...

Construction starts, and there are many changes that cost a lot of extra money. We juggle the changes within the contingency, so not everything can get done...

Finally we move in but the problems are still not resolved, so...

We struggle to operate in the facility—and problems continue to crop up. Then everybody realizes that we missed something important at the beginning..."

You can design your process to get away from this scenario. By handling these issues and getting clients more involved, more knowledgeable, and better able to make informed decisions, you can see major improvements in your business.

Paul Adams, AIA, an architect in Denver said it best: "All the big mistakes are made on the first day." If you focus your process on reducing or eliminating the first-day mistakes, you will see significant benefits.

We have found that you can do a much better job of getting your clients dependable, decision-making information, when and where they need it. You do this by looking closely at how you deliver projects and appropriately applying technology. We found that the trick is to manage project constraints from day one. This is how you can control the first-day mistakes.

A clear path

Technology and communications continue to compress our world. Today we buy something from our "local" computer store and they deliver it to our door from the other side of the world. In what seems like the blink of an eye.

Google.com, Expedia.com, and Amazon.com have revolutionized how we interact with the world. Yet, even in this new "flat" world, architects have not changed how they design and deliver their services. There are phenomenal savings and efficiencies to be had by those who embrace change and rethink their businesses to take advantage of this new world.

People have been trying forever to understand the impacts of technology on society. From the perspective of 2007, much of this discussion appears very distant and disconnected from integrated practice. In the 1970s, pioneers envisioned or invented many of the technologies that make BIM and integrated practice possible. Visionaries such as R. Buckminster Fuller and Alvin Toffler foretold much of the change. By 1975, management systems that integrated social and technical systems were well defined and in use in manufacturing. George Heery, William Caudill, and others redefined many of the construction delivery methods that we now consider "old-hat."

For many, building information modeling seems like another software solution. In this context, it is difficult to embrace the change. The benefits seem minor. Without understanding the issues and the underlying power of BIM, it is hard to see how it will benefit you personally. It is hard to see a clear path to success. However, done right, BIM can change your life for the better. Our goal is to show you how to do BIM right. Right now.

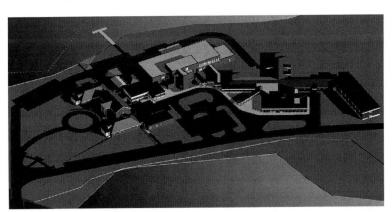

Crisfield, MD—McCready Memorial Hospital has used bim models for renovation, additions, master planning, environmental analysis, and strategic planning since 1993.

The methods detailed in this book are designed to help you use these actions to become an integrated practice, over time. As we move to the next phase in our exploration, we look at how you can provide value.

Action

As we explored how to make the change to integrated practice, we found that a successful process has to revolve around systems that value all team members. Work with clients, consultants, and your staff to ensure that they understand the goals and philosophy that drive the process. Steadily expand the circle of those who understand and believe in the change. When they understand how you deliver value, their performance is enhanced.

Some of the actions that lead to better understanding and successful integrated practice include:

- Increase the numbers of alliances with others focused on similar goals.
- Explore new and evolving technology.
- Design, test, and apply tools to manage information.
- Use innovation as a management tool to develop new insights, explore new roles, and understand new viewpoints.
- Build an environment fully engaged in positive change.
- Educate others to increase the understanding of integrated processes.
- Apply the right skills at the right time to the right elements.
- Consult and involve your supply chain in decision-making.
- Record information to confirm decisions or to create future value, not to track blame.

Integrated future

In the future, integrated practice will likely revolve around nationwide groups of firms that work cooperatively to achieve dramatic improvements in the built environment. They will create more sustainable and dependable projects that provide true value to all. Progressive cross-disciplinary organizations will achieve these benefits through systems that provide rules, standards, and relationships designed to produce superior results using BIM. Such organizations will empower firms of any size to work big, anywhere.

There have been early attempts at achieving such a goal. One such group, the Triglyph Architectural Organization successfully mobilized a national network of small firms with diverse skills, all using ArchiCad and an established set of standards. The Triglyph organization was a precursor to the types of organizations that BIM will create in the future.

In the United Kingdom, the Strategic Forum for Construction (SFC) has made strides in defining systems that reduce the fragmentation, duplication and adversarial relationships of their construction industry. They are working toward creating systems that foster cooperation, collaboration and mutual support. Their goal is to enable organizations to focus on shared goals and objectives without undermining their ability to advance and compete.

The SFC has deployed a Web-based tool called the *Integration Project Toolkit*. The Toolkit introduces the principles of integration and allows you to measure your 'integration maturity' against other users.

As practice concepts such as these develop, firms will be able to capitalize on strengths such as personal service and quick response. They will also have the versatility to become whatever their clients need, wherever and whenever they need it, while having large-firm tools, resources and networks available to them. The integrated practice of the future will turn-on-a-dime and bring the best-of-the-best to bear to solve problems, no matter how big or how small.

Now we will explore what organizations in the building industry could become in the near future.

Clans still at War!

For immediate release
November 2007 - Salisbury, MD

Clans oblivious to technology.

Despite huge productivity advancements across all industry sectors, the design and construction industry today continued its downward decline. Members of the Builder clan launched a surprise attack on the Owner clan, apparently unaware that the Design clan was preparing its own offensive against the Builders. This battle occurred days after the Designer clan suffered a bloody defeat at the hand of the Owner clan. All clans were observed fortifying their ancient dwellings. The adversarial conditions are nearing the point of self-destruction for the groups.

Some of the clans, however, are reporting magical image boxes appearing on their stone worktables. They say that they are fun to look at and they enjoy impressing other clansmen with what they can make them do. One clansman boasted, "We were able to completely replace our abacus!" Another admitted, "...We really don't understand why it's here."

New relationships

If Technology could talk it would scold, "What are you people waiting for!?!"

People have established social organizations for ten thousand years. From clans to countries, and ancient Mesoamerican ballgames to bowling leagues, every group came together because they shared values, had common needs, and agreed upon a strategy. They shared the risks and rewards of their endeavor.

Technology has evolved faster than people have. We now have to retool our social cultures in the building world to catch up and take advantage of the workhorse we have created.

In the not so distant future owners, builders, and designers, with the right technological knowledge, will establish a new social order. One based on strong common goals: Cost-effective facility development and operations.

New organizations

In an attempt to capitalize on owners' dissatisfaction with their services, many of today's builders and designers are attempting to modify current delivery methods. For the most part their efforts have been futile. The problems continue to get worse.

A new group of forward-thinkers has thrown out the old ways. They believe they should organize around the needs of all team members—designers, builders and owners equally. They believe that using common tools, systems and standards will lead to better collaboration. They will build trust and lead to a free flow of information and knowledge development. They will proactively create a long-term business strategy for future facility development and operations. They will insist that the risks and rewards accrue to all stakeholders.

The Facility Development and Operations (FDO) organization that they envision will be owner focused. It will include nationwide alliances of similar but non-competing owners. It will also include similar alliances of designers and builders specializing in the various aspects of these owners' industry.

FDO organizations will grow to become information-rich, relationship-driven institutions with a knowledge ecology that continuously creates evolutionary changes to the buildings they produce and operate.

New rules

New capabilities inconceivable a few years ago are reinventing the building industry. Trying to fit this new world into current socio/economic/legal pigeonholes will delay the progress. The silos of activity and information that now make up our world must be interconnected for the FDO to be successful.

The Facility Information Database will be a more powerful version of what we now call the building information model. The facility information database will be an integral part of the facility. It will remain "connected" to the project and will not used for any other purpose. The Facility Specific Alliance owns the database.

The FSA will be a unique legal entity, not unlike today's limited liability corporation, established and populated by the project's stakeholders (owner, constructor, and designer). It will be based on parameters set by the contract and responsible for designing, building, and operating the facility. The entity, along with the Facility Information Database, will remain permanently a part of the facility.

Performance and pre-established goals determine compensation. All members share the financial risks and rewards on a basis that closely aligns with their work effort, exposure to risk and responsibility.

Compensation will use a three-tiered payment strategy:

1. The cost of the work is always paid.
2. Overhead and profit paid if members meet all goals.
3. Bonuses paid if members exceed goals and as risk lessens.

A conflict free FID becomes the standard for performance during construction. The project is self-insured through the

The FDO organization of the future will structure their world like this:

Owner

The Owner determines new or modified facility needs via internal business operations. They establish the project program and budget—using tools and standards of the organization in partnership with the constructor and designer. The owner finances all aspects of the project including insurances. They actively participate as a member of the Facility Specific Alliance (FSA). They own and operate the building using its Facility Information Database (FID) and the FSA at completion.

Designer

The Designer creates the solutions, in partnership with the builder and owner. They facilitate, orchestrate and manage the Facility Information Database until building occupancy. The designer creates prototypes of the facility in collaboration with the facility alliance. They virtually confirm all requirements of the design through environmental simulations, space-time use analysis, visual simulations, code and program confirmation, schedule, financial feasibility, and construction analysis. They ensure that all consultants adhere to organization guidelines and contract. They actively participate as a member of the Facility Specific Alliance.

Constructor

The Constructor builds the proposed solution in partnership with designer and owner. They use and expand the facility information database; through the designer, for procurement, construction management, fabrications, temporary structures and site safety. The constructor establishes and uses material and labor supply chains, within the guidelines of the organization. They ensure that all sub-contractors, suppliers, and manufacturers adhere to organization guidelines and the project contract. They actively participate as a member of the Facility Specific Alliance.

bonus fund. No member, at any level, may sue another. Team members resolve mistakes between themselves and pay required costs from the bonus fund or overhead and profit fund.

The FSA supports its needs and advances its goals efficiently and equitably.

Open competition

People will start these organizations, but the natural laws of capitalism will shape them. Within this context, profits will be synonymous with healthy growth. Competition will be synonymous with improvement. As the organization grows and prospers, more members—owners, constructors and designers alike, will enter the group. Competition, both within the organization and from external sources, will cause some companies to leave and others to thrive.

The FDO organization does not worry about a member leaving with trade secrets or other information. The FDO is not about hoarding information. It is about processes, relationships and knowledge building. The members of the FDO organizations have *gotten over themselves*. They realize that everything they know is but a mouse click away on someone else's *magic image box*. Their value, and that of the organization, comes from how fast, how creatively and how accurately, new knowledge can be developed and brought to bear upon the unique problem at hand.

Lead change

Clan wars are not as farfetched as you may believe. The construction industry is fraught with infighting and adversarial relationships. It may be the only industry with a reduction in productivity since the advent of computerization.

Oversight

The FSA empowers and funds a "third party" oversight group that:

- Executes directions set by the organization (new programs, tools, marketing and business standards).
- Maintains communication among members of the organization.
- Manages support partners (software developers, material suppliers and others).
- Manages the Facility Specific Alliances.
- Establishes and controls conditions of membership.
- Mediates disputes.
- Facilitates positive organization growth.

Why has the building industry computerized if there is no productivity gain? Other industries have adapted to the changes wrought by technology and have improved the quality and effectiveness of their products. Something in the way the building industry does business needs to change.

It is easy to forget that much of what we take for granted now was revolutionary at one time. The way that we work today did not happen by accident. Today's approach came about because creative people applied creative ideas to solve problems. They took risks to get results and make the world a better place.

In the post-WWII years, Buckminster Fuller and Alvin Toffler envisioned many of the systems now considered standards of the industry. During the same period, Caudill Rowlett Scott and George Heery expanded the definition of construction management and the multidisciplinary predesign process. By the mid-1980s, commercial software to create

Clans Unite!

For immediate release
July 2010 - Salisbury, MD

In a remarkable turn of events, Owner, Designer and Constructor clans announced today a new organization based on open communication, trust and sharing. Recognizing that each of their three groups had risen from ancient tradition and now strive for a new classic order they called their organizational concept Triglyph.

Productivity is on the rise with a new kind of strength that is greater than the sum of its parts. A spokesperson for the organization said, "The true recipients of this new value proposition are the users of the facilities, the community and the environment."

More on this breaking story as the details prove out...and they will!

what we now know as building information models was in productive use. When you look at the seeds planted in the last half of the 20th century, you begin to realize that much of what they theorized is now happening. Many of their ideas now seem obvious. These visionary people and tools inform today's process and provide pointers to "best practices" and integrated practice implementation strategies.

Figuring out how to incorporate technology into the building industry is a big task. The industry is so widespread and includes so many players, that it is hard to wrap it into a tidy package. It is so diverse that it touches everything in our lives. It is hard to define, and when a problem is hard to define, it is hard to solve.

Finding solutions to problems within this complex system has always been difficult. Architects and other construction professionals have made incremental changes, trying to solve individual problems. Their improvements have tended to focus on one group or one client area. At times these solutions filtered through the industry. However, prior to building information modeling and integrated practice arriving

Robert A. Humphrey perhaps said it best when he said—"An undefined problem has an infinite number of solutions."

on the scene, few groups even attempted to find real solutions to the larger problems.

When people did most of the work by hand, it was relatively easy to fix problems. As the building industry has adopted more and more technological innovations, it has become harder and harder to make systemic repairs. Today, the industry faces problems of poor execution, poor cost controls, and a perception that traditional processes are deteriorating.

Technology has increased the pace and volume of change. Design firm resources to respond to these changes are limited. The number and complexity of building systems has reached a level that requires multiple experts in order to select workable solutions, much less the optimum solution. The sheer number of new building materials is becoming difficult to grasp. It is even more difficult to develop design expertise and experience with these new materials. Every day it becomes more difficult to respond to new needs.

Early in my career, I realized that architects had to change how they did business to respond to these issues. Continuing as usual was not a solution. It seemed like every time someone struggled to maintain the status quo, it signaled a failure to come. Patchwork solutions just were not working. There had to be a better and more efficient way to work in the world of tomorrow.

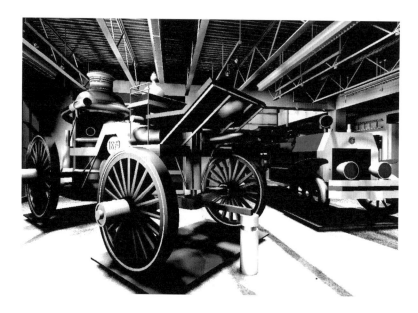

Salisbury, MD - Museum interior during concept design. Users create custom objects for nearly any real-world item. Even user created objects are intelligent and support early decision-making.

Beliefs

The beliefs that guide you today are the culmination of many years of experience and training. These beliefs are based on what you have been taught and learned as you worked your way up in the business. Your beliefs guide your actions and can change the way you do business, for the better. Your beliefs can also make your business stall and never reach its full potential.

No one can learn everything. The world is just too big and too complicated. By necessity, you can only become expert in a limited range of issues. This makes collaboration with many other people a necessity, not a luxury. The sheer volume of data that affects you everyday can be a blessing or a curse. By developing strategies for managing this data, you maximize its value in your life. You can either use the data or let the information inundate you.

Integrated practice using building information models to manage data offers you a way to manage these issues in your firm. The change will likely require you to reassess some of your beliefs. You can look at integrated practice as a new skill that requires training to master. It requires that you reassess many of the things that you know. It requires that you reconsider some of your closely held beliefs.

Success in any endeavor comes from how you apply your beliefs and values. By applying them consistently, you create your own way of doing things. The same is true in integrated practice.

The beliefs and values that drive successful integrated practice include:

- Design is part of everything you do.
- The process is managed by constraints.
- Design and implementation can work in parallel.
- Early decisions affect the quality of outcomes.
- Tradition and legacy systems must not overshadow good business decisions.
- Working together, you can define mutually beneficial objectives that create more value.
- Good communication and knowledge sharing build strong project teams.
- You are part of integrated supply networks that are critical to clients' success.
- It is not enough to have a good idea. Only when you act and implement can you make innovation happen day in and day out.

The concepts included in this list are not revolutionary. In fact, they likely make sense to you. They seem a bit obvious. However, have you really integrated these beliefs in how you work, every day?

Architects are known as creative problem solvers. Yet sometimes their closely held beliefs cause them to repeat errors and sub-optimize how they do business. An architect who applies the same level of creativity to business and delivery processes as he or she does to design, becomes a strong force in the economy.

Integrated practice offers significant benefits, to you and your clients. Changing how you look at projects and the building industry gives you many advantages. As you explore how the list above affects your beliefs, consider the advantages to a process that achieves more, faster while also improving relationships. You will find that it is well worth the effort.

Forewarned

Writer Miguel de Cervantes' succinct insight, "Forewarned is forearmed," still rings true over one hundred and ninety years later.

Little is totally new.

As obvious as it may seem, simply providing your clients with better early information makes it easier for them to see what lies ahead.

Helping your clients in this search starts with five broad principles:

Communication—Use technology to give immediate access. Clear and open communication is the first priority. Without this, nothing else is possible.

Integration—Optimize working practices, methods, and behaviors to get maximum value. Create a culture where the team is able to work together efficiently and effectively.

Interoperability—Build structures that capture everything. Then share the information. Eliminate repetition. Do your work once and use the information for many purposes.

Knowledge—Capture everything in dependable archives. Use real-world rules about how things relate to each other to improve efficiency. Use knowledge to eliminate the mundane and speed critical decisions. Pay attention to the details.

Certainty—Use everything at your disposal to make things clear. Reuse data to get the right information, at the right time, to those who must decide.

BIM is not

In the simplest terms, these five principles describe what BIM and integrated practice are all about. You focus on creating the most efficient and effective ways to support owners. You become more agile and more efficient. You become an asset and resource in the built environment value network.

Confusion creeps into the discussion of BIM for a variety of reasons. In the introduction to this book, we discussed the BIG BIM/little bim issue. The difference is where much of the confusion lies. The complexity of the subject, coupled with market driven self-interest leads to many of the misunderstandings. This is a new and evolving market and sometimes people are more interested in making a sale than in imparting the truth. The battle for dominance among vendors leads to messages designed to put products in the best light. Sometime reality gets lost in the hype. The confusion created is usually unintentional, but sometimes not. The best approach is to be wary and to question everything, no matter how plausible or enticing the message.

BIM is managing information to improve understanding. BIM is not CAD. BIM is not 3D. BIM is not application oriented. BIM maximizes the creation of value. Up, down, and across the built environment value network.

In the traditional process, you lose information as you move from phase to phase. You make decisions when information becomes available, not necessarily at the optimal time.

BIM is much different. The easiest way to understand BIM is to understand what BIM is not.

BIM is not a single building model or a single database. Vendors may tell you that everything has to be in a single model to be BIM. It is not true. They would be more accurate describing BIM as a series of interconnected models and databases. These models can take many forms while maintaining relationships and allowing information to be extracted and shared. The single model or single database description is one of the major confusions about BIM.

BIM is not a replacement for people. BIM is still a lot of hard work. By reducing the mundane, BIM lets you work smarter. It requires different training and a different mindset.

BIM will not automate you out of existence. You will always gather information. You will always process this information with your unique problem solving skills. You will always need to be a master of visual communications. However, you will do it with less effort.

BIM is not perfect. People input data into BIM. Because people are not perfect, sometimes they will incorrectly enter data. Since you enter information once, there is less chance for error. This allows you to capture knowledge easily and reduces repetitive input. Errors that creep in are easier to find, before they cause harm.

⚠ WARNING

THIS IS NOT A BUILDING INFORMATION MODEL. DOCUMENT MUST BE COORDINATED MANUALLY BEFORE USE.

By minimizing mundane tasks, BIM reduces errors.

BIM is not Revit (or ArchiCad, or Bentley). Those who do not understand the technology think that BIM and Revit mean the same thing. They are the same people who tell you that they use "CAD," when they really mean "AutoCAD." They make "Xerox" copies even when using a Minolta photocopier. Software companies do a wonderful marketing job. However, these programs are all wonderful bim solutions, not "the" BIM solution. You can use any of them and not be doing BIM at all.

BIM is not 3D. 3D software lets you model geometry. It is one of the great visualization tools. 3D modelers have greatly improved our ability to communicate ideas. In concept, 3D models are little more than lengths, widths, heights, and surface material images. With a 3D model, you still have to interpret what things mean, how they connect to other things and where they reside in space.

Building information models know all these. BIM knows how it relates to others. It is defined by standards. It can be shared. BIM is not a piece of software. It is not a 3D model. It is not a project phase. However, it can be any or all of these.

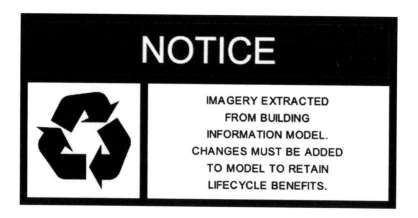

NOTICE

IMAGERY EXTRACTED
FROM BUILDING
INFORMATION MODEL.
CHANGES MUST BE ADDED
TO MODEL TO RETAIN
LIFECYCLE BENEFITS.

Images and graphic output is not BIM. They are views of the BIM database.

BIM does not have to be 3D. A spreadsheet can be BIM. One example is a simple address spreadsheet. It includes the names, street addresses, city, state, zip code, and perhaps the Web site addresses. The data is in a standardized format. It is a useful tool, but not yet BIM. When you import this data into Google Earth, each line of the spreadsheet is analyzed and placed (georeferenced) in context. The data takes on new dimensions and power. You can share it, add to it, and use it for comparisons. The data from the spreadsheet interacts with the complexity, and interrelationships of today's organizations and environment. It becomes BIM.

BIM is not complete. Some people argue that all standards and tools must be in place before BIM can be successful. Others assume that BIM is not possible unless everyone in the process is involved. They are wrong. Standards and defined processes are certainly necessary—in the long view. Involving everyone in the building industry is certainly the long-range goal. The fact is that today, BIM is being applied effectively. BIM is increasing efficiency and leveraging our ability to support owners. BIM is profitable.

If you cannot share your data, it has limited value.

bim solutions have common characteristics: they create digital databases and allow use of data by collaboration; they coordinate the data to reflect changes to any item throughout the database; and they capture and preserve knowledge for reuse.

As you start to integrate your projects, remember that **Communication—Integration—Interoperability—Knowledge—Certainty** drive BIM.

Your first task is to consider how to use these five principles in your practice. By then understanding the inefficiencies in your practice, you can find BIM solutions to fix them. Take it a step at a time. You will make the changes in the way that works best for you and your clients.

You will likely see benefits in different areas than others see. Your projects require any number of design processes. You can improve any of them with a bim solution. Once you start to improve your processes and begin to see success, you can then widen your reach. If you are like others that have taken this path, you will over time, find yourself integrating more processes. You will create greater value in the built environment.

PART II

FRAMEWORK
FOR
SUCCESS

CHAPTER 3

Four phases to integration

Ocean City, MD—Analysis begins with the first prototype. Shading and daylighting are two studies simplified by bim models.

IT IS HARD TO FIND THE BEST way to communicate integrated practice concepts. Everyone hears messages and receives information a little differently. There are many different learning styles. As you explore how to implement the process, you will find new and innovative ways to communicate your message. Take every opportunity to reinforce the concepts in your network of staff, consultants, and clients.

A squishy fish tale

A few years ago, we worked with an airport planner, Hirsh Associates, on an airport terminal. The next December Joel Hirsh sent us a stress airplane tagged with "Celebrating 20 Years of Hard Analysis for a Squishy Industry." It was a cute and different way to send a holiday greeting. The cards that we received that year went in the trash; the airplane is still on our shelf. It made a lasting impression.

The next September, we had our annual discussion about holiday mailings. As usual, we looked for ways to differentiate ourselves. Frank Brady, one of our 4Site Managers, suggested that we do "something like that—pointing at Joel's airplane." Leisl Ashby, a young architect, pulled out a stress fish that she had received from a supplier—"Why not do fish? Why not play on the ATLANTIC theme? We could even do different fish every year." The Design Atlantic Ltd squishy fish was born.

Right now, you are asking yourself—"What do squishy fish have to do with integrated practice?" Squishy fish have everything to do with it.

The fish are a mnemonic, a memory aid, to help communicate our corporate creed—*We reduce your stress by getting you early, dependable knowledge about your project.* The fish tie us to our roots—the Delmarva Peninsula, situated right between the Atlantic Ocean and the Chesapeake Bay. They are collectable. You can build your collection of squishy fish over time—as we help you to do for your facilities.

In early December 1998, we sent out our first squishy fish. Every year we send out new colors of fish. Last holiday season, we sent out our tenth anniversary fish. Our friends collect them. Our clients and friends identify us with our colorful fish. Recently a longtime client, quipped—"You better send me another fish"— when he heard what his new project would cost.

We have clients who call us for extras if we send only one. They are good conversation pieces. They are memorable.

We hand them out at interviews and they help get jobs. We hand them out at shows and they get us leads. We use them as stuffing in proposals. We hand them out anywhere we go.

Squishy fish are integrated!

A couple of years ago, we were hired to help a fire company develop a strategic plan. If you have ever worked with volunteer firefighters, you know how passionate they are about their fire companies. When they are saving you from your burning house, their passion is a great and wonderful thing. When they are participating in a planning process, their passion takes some serious management.

As part of the process, they decided to hold a three-day retreat. The first day the group nearly became physical—they agreed to disagree about almost everything. The squishy fish suddenly took on a role that we had never envisioned. The fish are light and act like soft snowballs when you throw them. The group began to use the fish to take out their frustrations, by throwing fish instead of fists.

The squishy fish diffused the tensions. They provided a non-damaging outlet for the group to begin to reach a consensus. It looked a lot like a bunch of kids in a snowball fight. The squishy fish fight actually helped us reach agreement. By the end of the third day, the group created a strategic plan they could all buy into and support. The fish helped.

Do more with less

How do you assess a client's needs and then arrive at a design that solves his or her problem? If you are like most architects, you began to wrestle with this question early in your training and career. As you became more competent, the question took up less of your attention. You integrated your personal solution into your way of doing work. It became a part of your life.

Sometimes you have to step back and reconsider questions like this. Over time the things that we have come to take for granted can grow stale. A new look at old ideas can reinvigorate your process.

Projects under control

In 1996, we revisited the question of finding better ways to apply technology to leverage architectural practice. Since then we have tested thousands of software and hardware tools.

Individually—and as part of systems. All with the goal of finding the "best" and most profitable solutions. Some we kept and use today. Some we discarded for a variety of reasons. Some never worked, some worked for a while, and some are wonderful.

We performed these explorations in a real-world setting. A functioning and profitable architectural practice. Ours were not "ivory-tower" tests. Rather we used the tools on real projects.

If they worked,—great. If not, we moved on and looked for the next possibility. This was a ten-year exploration.

All but three of those years were profitable. The three "bad" years were caused by people errors and bad teaming decisions. We learned volumes about how systems for managing technology and systems for managing people differed in those years.

We came to the realization that owner needs had to drive the process. Even at the technology level. We had to become owner driven. We searched and found the one thing that clients most want from our services. The concept was simple.

Owners want their projects to be under control. They want to know where they are going.

Technology gives us the tools to make it happen.

When you help clients by providing control that is more dependable you become of more value in the process. Working to create this kind of value is not a new thing. It has been talked about for generations. Most firms likely include similar words in their mission statements. Nevertheless, how many can really do it, consistently?

In graduate school, I was lucky enough to study with Buckminster Fuller and Alvin Toffler. It is easy to forget that they were talking about this very issue well before 1970. Perhaps it has taken this long for technology to "catch up" with their theories.

Their ideas still make sense today. The world has changed, yet much of what they theorized is now possible. Many of their ideas are now in the mainstream. Their ideas continue to offer clues to the best ways to use technology to make the world a better place.

Buckminster Fuller's Operating Manual for Spaceship Earth, written in 1969, is a precursor and roadmap for what BIM is letting us do—write the Operating Manual for the Built Environment. In his explorations of how humanity can survive on the planet Earth, he championed doing more with less and taking a comprehensive view of the world. His concept of "Comprehensive Anticipatory Design Science" is now practical—using information-modeling technology. He predicted the overlapping of specialties that is standard to integrated practice. Today you really can use technology, filtered by your innate abilities, to look at our world in a more comprehensive way.

Fuller was responsible for many of today's concepts in sustainability. He taught that you could use technology to anticipate and solve problems with fewer resources. By breaking down the built environment and social issues that impact upon it into bite-sized pieces, you can implement his ideas. Building on his work, you can integrate technology to "do more with less." BIM is the process that allows you to implement his ideas.

The Path to integration chapter later in this book details some of the tools that are making Fuller's ideas a reality.

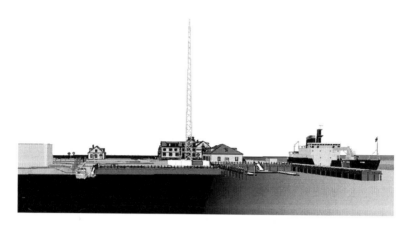

Atlantic City, NJ—Facilities become an integral part of the owner's business decision-making process. This view is extracted from an as-built information model. Use bim models to archive both facility and business process information.

Manage better

Architects are at their best when taking complex information and synthesizing it to create innovative solutions. Architects are realizing that it is virtually impossible to catch up to the trends unless they develop new practice paradigms. It is no longer adequate to replace drafting by hand with drafting by computer.

Architects can no longer allow vendors to push them into an applications focus—in order to sell more software. Integrated practice and building information modeling are not about buying the right software. They are about adopting processes and finding the best tools to deliver the highest value to your clients.

Move toward methods that make information easily available, in formats that will talk to each other and, in a shared environment that mirrors the real world. Become more. Become an information architect.

Architects have always managed data. 2D CAD solutions were a first step toward automating the process. In hindsight, these solutions actually increased the level of error and lack of project control that plagues the construction industry.

Since these files are not interoperable and require complex management controls—they increase the potential for error. The crisp and "finished document" look gives a false sense of quality, rather than providing improved coordination and clarity, as has often been promised.

Although it is impossible to predict how a building will be altered over time, it is certain that each renovation will start with understanding existing conditions. Because the data is already in place in a BIM system, the revision process is more efficient. You no longer worry about lost or unavailable documents, or data that someone has entered incorrectly.

The advantage of BIM is that all building data is embedded and can be accessed throughout the facility's life cycle. From that data, architects can accurately simulate the building in its present or proposed future state—in context. Using this data, you start with better, more current data about a facility. With the initial data entry process all but eliminated, so are the mistakes that invariably accompany manual input.

Because of this, significantly fewer people are required to maintain a higher level of quality. Because you derive most of the necessary building information from this data—you can automatically handle a much larger portfolio. This data represents the state of the facility and its connections to the built environment value network. Since each tiny "bit" of data represents a discrete part of the whole, you minimize repetition. You are no longer required to sort out multiple versions of the same information. This eliminates much of the confusion and potential for error.

Earlier in the Squishy fish tale, we discussed how a fire company's retreat benefited from the process. At the same time as the retreat, we were finishing two buildings for the same client. When the projects were complete, the client returned 10% of the construction budget to their accounts. The contractor, his subcontractors, the architect and the engineers all made a profit. The project finished on time and under budget in a market where few projects even come close to their goals.

This happened because of an integrated process using building information models.

A few weeks after the project was complete, we received a trophy marlin from the client. The marlin still lives on the wall in our reception area and proudly announces us as "Information Architects" to everyone who visits.

Value network

Making your clients' lives better, saving them money, and staying profitable is what integrated practice is all about. When you create a process that helps you to do better work, more efficiently—you become more successful. You provide greater value.

Creating an integrated practice does not happen overnight. It is not a matter of switching off the lights after a day of working the traditional way and coming in the next morning to a new, better approach. It requires planning and organization. It is a change management effort.

You will find your unique combination of skills, tools and experiences to make the switch in your firm. At Design Atlantic Ltd, we created 4SiteSystems to highlight the change.

Many times, architects let constraints manage how they do business; they are not proactive. 4SiteSystems sprang from the ideas of R. Buckminster Fuller, Alvin Toffler, George Heery, and William Caudill. It built on Goldratt's Theory of Constraints and the Toyota Production System (TPS). 4SiteSystems changes how we look at projects and our place in the built environment.

Proven management theory grounds the process. It builds on the best and most successful parts of traditional architectural practice and construction processes.

The effort begins with information and management.

Collect and hoard information management solutions. In a world of Web2.0 you have to be an aggregator. You have to keep up with the tools that are developing every day. The same is true in the world of bim tools.

We initially created the 4SiteSystems process to react to this environment of change and to establish a common vocabulary for integrating these solutions into our practice. As it developed, 4SiteSystems became an integrated process and framework to design projects using the latest technologies. The process has been tested, prototyped, and used successfully for over ten years. The process makes building information modeling possible today.

The process occurs within four continuous "phases" that represent the cycle of facilities—from cradle to cradle. The process fosters a holistic view of projects. Where architects have traditionally focused on the middle ground, represented by design and construction, 4SiteSystems pushes a longer and more sustainable view. By broadening the focus to include a focus on "pre-design" and "post-construction," it forces greater consideration of the "big picture." This works to minimize expedient decisions.

Architects know that their clients are concerned about more than designing and constructing buildings. Yet, the "normal" design process does little to support long-term business and operations. Many owner concerns related to poor documentation, cost overruns, and other problems occur because of this narrow view.

There are clear advantages for owners who work with architects who think long term. When presented with the option, owners quickly see why an integrated process gives them better and earlier decision-making support and saves them money in the end. Owners, at little or no additional cost, end up with a more efficient process and facilities that are more effective over the long run.

The process focuses on managing cost constraints and blending:

- the architect's ability to synthesize information,
- construction management and design/build strategies and,
- emerging information technologies.

The process uses parametric models, cost control systems, and project and facilities management databases working together to produce a high level of project control and information resources. These tools permit realistic, virtual tours at the earliest stages of design.

The process invites "test fitting" of program functions, design features, facility operations, budgets, and even disaster recovery. Using bim tools, the process advances to facilitate quantity takeoffs, analyses, and multiple delivery systems. With 4SiteSystems, architects are doing a more diverse mix of projects, quickly and without sacrificing efficiency, even in "one-off" situations.

Initiate Phase

During the Initiate Phase, it is critical that you properly envision the project. With the correct strategy and vision for the project, the phases that follow become easier to manage and more successful. You focus on minimizing the "first-day" mistakes.

This focus on early certainty did not spring from thin air.

From our experiences, we knew that owners perceive that Agency Construction Managers (ACM) consistently solve their problems. The same is widely held to be true for Design/Builders. They thrive because they focus on the owners' interests. These professionals seem to move into positions that allow them to control projects more easily than architects. Is this because owners trust them to work in their best interests?

To understand what makes agency construction managers so successful, we deconstructed how they work. We did the same evaluation of design/builders. Why do owners go directly to construction managers and design/builders? What do they offer that makes owners call them first?

The groundwork laid by George Heery, Caudill Rowlett Scott, and CM Associates takes on new importance when viewed in the context of integrating practice and early decision-making. Along with a small group of other design and construction professionals, they pretty much created the profession of construction management. They sought to correct the same issues that concern today's building owners. By identifying problems early, in a client-centered way, they changed how architects and contractors delivered projects over the past thirty years. They improved results for many owners.

By controlling risks, costs, and time, they developed improved project outcomes for those who embraced the process. The procedures and philosophies that they created provide the most stable starting point for the future of integrated practice. Even if you did no more than integrate the processes that they developed, you would help your clients have more certainty of outcomes and smoother, more efficient projects.

Today, technology lets you do things that were possible only for the largest firms at the time that Heery, CRS, and CM Associates created their processes. Integrated practice and BIM give you the tools to take their ideas to a much higher level.

Communication tools

First, let's look at project communications tools.

Communication is essential to integrated practice. Without tools that simplify communication and allow owners to make decisions early, it is difficult to minimize errors and keep everyone in the loop. We have found that this requires two complementary systems.

One is a second-generation Internet-hosted service— entirely Web based. The other is an internal database.

The real trick is to unify the best available resources to create an overall package that allows you to easily pull marketing materials, manage office correspondence, manage the design process, manage reference materials and research, manage libraries, manage model servers, administer construction (or manage construction), manage facilities after construction, and help owners manage their facility portfolio.

Ocean City, MD - Prototype during predesign. Prototypes contain usable data from the beginning. Use this information to help your clients make more informed, early decisions.

Every project starts with a project Web site. All project communications flow through this site.

We use 37Signals' suite of Web-based collaboration tools. We deploy these tools and make them available to the client and all team members from day one. 37Signals takes what we believe to be a unique approach. Their products are a study in simplicity. They realize that most collaboration failures come from unclear communications. They make project communications as clear and as simple as possible.

We use Basecamp (www.basecamphq.com) for project communications, Highrise (www.highrisehq.com) for client resource management and Campfire (www.campfirenow.com) for real-time group chat. All of these products are databases that let us control our clients' data. These products serve up Really Simple Syndication (RSS) feeds that allow everyone to stay in the information "loop." They send reminders, and keep the entire team current with all project communications. This technology has gotten so inexpensive and so mature that there is no excuse to delay or charge for this level of support.

We use email for noncritical communications only. Without major effort and expensive server based solutions, email does not support the level of communications and collaboration that integrated practice requires. Email permits too much uncertainty. Too many things fall through the cracks with email. Communications are too critical, so we take a different approach.

We also use Arch Street Software's Portfolio Digital Practice Tools (www.arch-street.com) for architect-specific project management documentation. Portfolio Prime databases house ALL internal project documentation (letters/transmittals/forms), from initial client contact through punch lists. It is the closest thing to a functional "paperless" office product that we have found. Unfortunately, we still get paper from contractors and owners, so we have kept a few file cabinets.

Other products are on the market to handle this load. However, we have found that on a cost, productivity, and usability basis, Portfolio wins every time.

Using two database systems is a bit more complicated than switching to an all-in-one database. After testing many products, running cost analyses, working with customized solutions and falling victim to a lot of hype and false promises; 37Signals' and Arch Street's databases stand out. Today they are the best combination for our practice, so they are what we use. Tomorrow, that may change.

One truth of integrated practice is that there are always issues that fall outside of any system. You have to adapt and fill the holes. You have to work with more than one package to cover all the bases. The AIA's electronic contract documents and financial management systems are two examples of holes that you must fill. Perhaps someday someone will integrate everything into a truly functional architectural practice system. To us, this remains the holy grail of integrated practice. Perhaps a time will come when everything will go together into one simple and easy-to-use database. Until then...

Understand needs

Analyze, organize and understand the process.

Pulling together a team to design a client's project is second nature to most architects. Creating procurement processes that result in the correct contractors is not an unusual problem either. Neither is a new issue.

There are two new issues:

1. Obviously, not all architects or consultants will be conversant with BIM. This will create gaps in your integrated project teams. Until integrated practices become universal, these gaps in the process will be a fact of life. Design your processes to manage around them.

2. Integrated practice creates new and unexpected needs. These needs require new types of experts. A few of these experts will be familiar with the tools and processes. Most will not. Design your new processes to accommodate, coach and support experts from many specialty areas.

Much of the work done in the Initiate Phase is the same as for any project—traditional or integrated. You still have to initiate agreements, retain consultants, survey sites, review programs, and generally become familiar with the client and his or her project.

The difference comes when you change your overall focus from merely designing projects to getting the owner certainty about his or her project. **The first is architect process focused and the second is owner process focused.**

As you progress through this book, you will get a better idea of the importance of this difference. This subtle change in focus is critical to integrated practice.

You use a variety of tools to accomplish the change.

We will discuss some of the tools and processes that make this possible, in later chapters. Rules-based systems, such as the Onuma Planning System (OPS), are the leaders in this area. Few will have used such systems at this time.

Other tools, such as bim modelers, schedulers, spreadsheets, and programs such as SketchUp! and Visio, are likely already in your toolbox today. Any and all of them are used in developing early decisions data. As we focus on rapid decision support, one methodology stands out—**mind maps.**

Mind mapping is a visual thinking methodology that closely mirrors the unstructured processes that take place early in projects. Mind maps allow you to represent connections between information. They streamline meetings, note taking and decision-making. They dramatically improve your ability to organize and present the complex interrelationships that we manage. They allow you to structure unstructured data, classify information, problem solve, and quickly make decisions, in a collaborative environment. A solid mind-mapping tool, such as Mindjet's MindManager, makes project and process planning easier, improves communication, and accelerates the process.

Automate

We can automate much. But not everything.

Integrated practice will always be about people. There will always be "personal intervention" in the process. Automation of the process reduces the mundane and lets you focus on critical issues. Automation of the process allows you to deliver "just-in-time" decision-making—even for the smallest project.

Early information is important.

Some time ago, we were retained to convert a basement area in a law office. We had known the attorneys for a long time. In fact, we had done the interiors for their original offices—before BIM. At this scale most experienced architects would give the client a quick top-of-the-head assessment of the project, write up an agreement and start detailed design.

We start even tiny projects with a subtle difference.

Now we work differently. We first got authorization for a minimal validation process. We did a quick site survey and assembled a basic bim model designed to act as a data container. The model was nothing more than a zone object capable of holding areas, furniture, finishes and other project data.

The project was too small to warrant a more complete prototype model. From this information, we created a cost model using parametric, rules-based data maintained in our system. The cost model responded to the project's scope, quantities, timelines and other client requirements.

The entire process took place in a morning.

We then sat down with the attorneys and went over the project logic. They understood the issues and cost risks. They could now decide how to proceed, with good facts. They could move forward with certainty. They had the data to look at other options.

They became an active participant in the design decision-making, before they had to invest schematic and design development dollars. We could have given them our informed opinion. Instead, we gave them facts to help them make decisions.

This is a small example of the types of activities that occur in the Initiate Phase of every project.

Quickly making clear and organized information available to clients early is how we use an integrated process. This happens before the normal design process even begins. This is where the biggest benefits exist. This is where we can make the biggest impact. This is where we can structure to be successful throughout the process.

This is what drives an integrated practice. Through a truly collaborative process that recognizes the value of team members and works to achieve the high performance and economic value of the process, we achieve owner strategic goals and create a safer, better-managed world for those who follow.

Design Phase

Prototype with just the right data

The Design Phase brings to bear the tools for managing the design process. In this phase, you refine project information controls to reduce repetition that might occur in later phases of the process. You use these controls to be more efficient and productive in planning and design processes. In this phase, you may also tailor the project's bidding documents to the project's goals based on current "best-practice" methodologies.

Building information models form the containers to hold project information. They serve as links to the built environment value network. They also provide the linkages to relationships and processes. These models archive all project data.

Someday, when integration is widespread in the building industry, these models will closely reflect real-time and real-world conditions. Today, we plant the seeds for that future.

Today, you will start most of your models from scratch. You are creating models that will become permanent archives of projects. Information in these archives should be accurate. Realizing this long-term goal, you should build accurate and complete models from day one. This is a place where quality should trump quantity.

Adding too much data, too early is not economical. In practice, you do not have the information, time, or budgets to recreate the real world in the virtual world. Certainly not at the start of projects. If you are doing BIM, your models will never be complete. Models grow over time. Design a system that creates prototypes with "just enough" data to support the current need.

Add the data needed for the current use. Nothing more.

Doing BIM effectively means that you have to keep people in the process. Use your expertise to guide the process. Do not hand the responsibility for models off to untrained or inexperienced staff. Someone must be knowledgeable and capable of understanding the big picture and then making sure that any inconsistencies are managed correctly. As knowledge-based systems become widely available, you will be able to automate more of the process. Until then, it depends on your expertise—as it always has.

Because of this, models develop best in a step-by-step prototyping process that adds the correct data, at the proper time to support the decision-making process. With a mature bim modeling solution, each prototype stage becomes more complete and contains much more information than any traditional "flat" solution. Much of the information happens almost without effort. With a product that automates much of the tedious and repetitive work, creation of phased-in prototypes is both practical and profitable.

You create the first prototypes in the Initiate Phase. At that level, the prototype serves to define the scope of the project. It establishes a framework that contains all of the parameters for a successful project. It supports decision-making.

As the process moves forward, prototypes become more and more complete. Prototypes at the Design Phase define the design solution. They typically contain data that allows you to deliver documentation required for public bid of design/build projects. Compared to the "traditional" documents process, these prototypes represent 40-70% complete Construction Document data. Prototypes in later phases build up to include design/bid/build data, construction support data, and facilities management data.

Prototype models and intelligent objects allow any level of prototype to function up or down the system (i.e., you can use an Initiation Phase prototype for procurement of design/build services. You can extract construction documents from a Design Phase prototype, etc.). Since a well-planned prototyping process eliminates repetitive work, you smooth out your internal process and work more economically.

Transition

Some pundits are sending the message that architects are in no way even close to applying BIM technology. The truth is that on the academic—"spit out an answer without human intervention" level—they are right. On the level where you achieve major improvements to projects, get highly improved information, and improve outcomes for owners, the naysayers are not even close—because you can do it now.

The greatest benefits from integrated practice will come when we can share data with others—both in the design and construction process. Today, there are few engineers or contractors working in this environment. However, you can say the same of architects. Too few professionals in all disciplines have embraced the technology. As more owners demand integrated services and more professionals move to support them, this will change.

For now, create a strategy for integrated practice, knowing that many of your consultants and contractors are now learning of the issue. Within 4SiteSystems, we use a threefold strategy for handling this issue.

First, use engineers and contractors who understand where you are headed. If they "get it" they will likely change over time, to work in an integrated process. They have to be willing to learn and to start the change themselves. They have to be prepared to commit to adopting the process as interoperable engineering and virtual construction tools become readily available. Reaching this point with a consultant or a contractor requires a commitment to establishing a long-term relationship. It requires your willingness to commit to education and to clearly defining your requirements. Since you will be changing the "traditional" process, they will have to learn how best to provide input and support the process at the proper times.

Second, reconcile yourself to accept and output 2D non-bim formats to support consultants and contractors. You do not have to like it. Today you probably have to do it.

These files, by their very nature create redundant work. Fortunately, bim design tools are very competent at translations to major flat formats. You lose much (if not all) of the intelligence. Nevertheless, the geometry remains correct and the engineers and contractors get what they need to do their jobs. The sheet layout features of bim tools are good at incorporating flat formats into documentation sets. Flat formats give you information in the form of linework, geometry, and text only. They normally do not contain interchangeable or intelligent data to allow analysis or information sharing.

Third, many of the benefits for both architects and owners come from using integrated practice in a design/build mode. In this approach, the comprehensive vision represented in the prototype model defines the performance requirements to assure compliance by design/builders. The architectural concept is test fitted and evaluated using these early stage prototypes. Use this ability to reduce or eliminate the uncertainties that force bidders to embed contingencies. Use the prototype system to give the design/builder certainty from which to price and build your projects.

Today, few engineers are working in this manner. Because of this, design/builders must often rely on performance criteria that may or may not describe the ideal solution for a specific project. This is a compromise, required for this delivery method, at this time. As more engineers develop an integrated engineering design process, their systems will also be test fitted within the prototype.

If your design engineers are not working in an integrated manner, their performance criteria documents will continue to be the weak point in the process. You are pushing an open-ended responsibility for systems' design onto the design/builder's team, if engineering performance requirements are not integrated. Properly managed and contracted this scenario can allow the design/builder freedom within a defined framework. However, in most cases, this is counter to the goal of establishing certainty of outcomes that is an underlying principle of integrated practice.

We find new opportunities by assisting owners with this type of problem. Acting as design/build consultants, we work with owners to maximize the effectiveness of public bid design/build projects. We help them to minimize confusion and uncertainty in their requests for proposals.

We have had to rethink many of the services that we once sought from consulting engineers, in this mode. Ideally, the design/build consultant's engineers develop performance requirements for systems and then integrate and test them within the model. In practice, we find this level of integration is still a goal. We use the best design engineers that we can find and then test fit critical items only, rather than testing entire systems.

In many markets today, the entire design/builder team is NOT functional in BIM. You therefore lose the long-term advantage that comes from a fully integrated process, when you hand off the project to the design/builder. If the design/builder's team is not BIM proficient, the benefits effectively stop at this point.

In this scenario, the owner receives superior bid outcomes but gives up long-term benefits. The short-term benefits still make the process valuable. However, much of the value to owners comes during operations.

A partial solution is for the design/build consultant to maintain project models and project records in a parallel process. This parallel process lets the owner maintain the long-term benefits, although at additional cost. This is an expedient only. Even with design/build, your goal should be to contract with teams that can integrate with the process.

Construct Phase

The Construct Phase is about maintaining close and collaborative arrangements with the professionals who get projects built. The integrated process requires you to be very adaptable in the Construct Phase.

At a basic level, the goal is to improve communications and understanding to make traditional relationships work more effectively. You can accomplish this through improved decision-making, rapid processing of submittals, and a better understanding of cost and scheduling issues.

- The tools focus on monitoring construction within a collaborative process, if you have a traditional contract administration role. The project budget, validated in earlier phases, is coordinated with the contractor's schedule-of-values and becomes the framework for monitoring actual costs.

- In a minimally integrated construction environment, you work to leverage the traditional requirements and maintain building operations and maintenance data within the prototype model for use in the Manage Phase.

- In a more integrated situation, the goal is to provide constructors with higher-level support to improve their ability to manage the project. This involves prototypes to allow conflict checking, support for computer-assisted manufacturing of components, and 4D and 5D support.

Changing the process creates new opportunities.

Once owners and contractors understand the power and simplicity of the process, they cast architects into new and unexpected roles. You may find yourself in program management roles. You may transition from working for the owner to working for the contractor as the process develops.

Changing the process requires you to support new areas. Position yourself to take advantage of them.

Communications

Web-based project management becomes the focus of information flow among all Construct Phase team members. We use 37Signals' Basecamp to manage the information flow. This level of access minimizes excuses and focuses everyone on taking responsibility and getting the job done. All communications flow through this site, giving several advantages:

- All communications are date stamped. All uploads are version controlled. You minimize or eliminate information handling issues.

- Task assignments and Milestones with reminders, to minimize the "oops factor."

- Team members' contact information is available to everyone.

- Real-time archived Chat allows for retaining and sharing conversations across the team.

- Writeboards give the ability to create text documents collaboratively.

The only disadvantages that we have experienced from expanding the level of project communications, comes from those who do not understand the process. Or, from those who understand it and choose to continue working the way they always worked in the past. The problems that occur usually revolve around a team member's refusal to allow subcontractor access to team communications tools. When this happens, we begin to see decisions made out-of-context and the traditional communications problems that have plagued projects over the years.

Delivery

The integrated process is not limited to a single construction delivery method. Use the process for all delivery methods.

The largest benefits come from delivery approaches that allow the most interaction between owner, contractor, and architect. 4SiteSystems has proven to offer the greatest benefits for projects completed using bridged design/build and agency construction management.

Bridged design/build allows you to test fit and validate the project. You then communicate the results to design/build bidders at a very high level. This works to eliminate many of the "unknowns" that drive much of the cost variation in design/build. A high level of information about owner requirements coupled with clear communications results in very successful design/build projects.

The underlying concepts in the process are very similar to those used by many of today's most successful agency construction managers (ACM).

Because of this similarity, you will find that you can allocate responsibilities to focus on the firm best able to deliver each part of the project. The architect test fits the owner's requirements, using the prototype to minimize the "unknowns." The ACM then develops the cost model. They take on the responsibility for managing the cost constraint, by controlling the project's contingency. The architect provides rapid processing of submittals, communications systems, and facilities management support.

Manage Phase

Teaming BIM with Computer-Aided Facility Management (CAFM) seems like a marriage made in heaven.

Traditionally, architecture and facility management are entirely separate tasks in the life cycle of a building. Recognizing that owners require more than planning and design services to create and care for their buildings on a continual basis, you can better serve your clients.

At this stage, you have created highly detailed digital models that are usable for operations, running simulations, and planning for the facility's life. You store all of the building data in bim model files directly linked to a series of Web-enabled database files accessible throughout the building's life cycle. These models become archives for facility information from multiple sources. They build up over time. As facility use data accumulates, the models become more and more valuable as management and planning tools.

There are advantages to working with people who think long-term and work to solve long-term problems.

They are constantly looking to owners for insight into their facilities. They learn more about owners' business needs and become more valuable.

When they decide to incorporate Web-based facility management into their services, they begin to level the cyclical nature of the design business.

There have been problems getting owners and selection boards to see the advantages of an integrated approach. To some owners, the question is, "What's the big deal?" As these owners see it, any architect can do the same things that you do with bim, no matter what approach they use. Owners, therefore, see little or no advantage to themselves—no savings in cost and no reason to get in the middle of architects' process disputes.

> No matter how many fly-thrus you produce, how many 3D views you make available, or how quickly you turn documents around, some owners believe that all architects can do that.

Integrating facility management changes this equation in a big way. The owner can now see direct operational advantages that do not come from the traditional architect's process. With something to gain personally, the owner can see that your approach saves him or her money. The owner ends up with an easier-to-manage facility, after you go on to the next engagement.

You can truly begin to sell managing the information that is inherent in the BIM model. Working with owners to create long-term solutions gives you insight into better operations and maintenance of their facilities. Long-term management of information to support the entire facility life cycle creates the opportunity for the owner to have a major impact on financial performance.

This approach saves money for the life of the asset. Owners can see why integrated practice firms give them better and earlier decision-making information and save them money in the end. Owners can now, at little or no additional cost, end up with a more efficient process and facilities that are more effective.

CHAPTER 4

Plan your future

Extensive libraries of intelligent objects are commercially available. Users create special objects, such as this 1879 Steam Pumper, as required during the process

INTEGRATING TECHNOLOGY into your practice is a business decision. Like any other business decision, you can choose to do it or not. Over time, your decision will enable you to benefit from evolving technology—or not.

Implementing BIM into the day-to-day workings of a profitable office requires a level of process change that some find difficult to justify. The changes often run up against basic design and office management beliefs and training. There are however, proven ways to maximize the benefits of the change.

Changing workflows and integrating technology is a change management process. Clearly defining your expectations for each step will make it possible for your entire team to work in concert to make the changes to your business, effectively and efficiently.

Before computers came along, an architect's work revolved around information management. We called it something else, but it was still information management. We had to marshal all the possibly relevant data and then sort, filter, and massage it into useful project information. In the past, we accomplished this with notes, books, Rolodexes, and stacks of index cards. Creating a design solution requires you to manage massive amounts of information. Are you doing it efficiently? Can you reuse the information? Are you reinventing the information for every project?

If you are like most architects, you have already spent money and time to automate your office. You use word processors, spreadsheets, and Computer Aided Design and Drafting programs to improve specific tasks. You have trained your staff to use these tools.

Rather than looking at integration from a systems perspective, you have focused on task automation. With a task-based approach, you likely ended up inputting the same information over and over—a time-consuming and error-prone practice. The problem becomes especially severe when you consider that fully computerized firms use a dozen or more different applications, from electronic time sheets to digital image libraries, each with its own database.

Create clear and understandable information to help you make the decision to change. Step back and look at the "first principles" that drive your business. Define your business goals. Evaluate your capabilities and understand how your clients will perceive the value of the change.

Decisions

You will make decisions based on many factors. Some will be internal - What do you want to do? Some will be external - What do your clients need? Some may be for the greater good - What is best for the profession?

Some of the questions to ask include:

- Can we work in a way that better supports client needs and concerns?
- Who will own the information in our database?
- Who owns the copyright to the model? Does anything change with the design copyright?
- Who will manage the model?
- Who will have access to the model database?
- If BIM is so good, why aren't more architects using it?
- Doesn't everyone use AutoCAD? Or Revit? Or Bentley? Or ArchiCad?
- If we use cost to manage the process, won't we destroy the design process?
- Can we do better design and eliminate the after-the-fact fixes?

The advantage of integrated practice is that you can work with your systems to store all of your data in reusable formats. Your data can make it easier to work with others. Your data can let you provide more value to your clients. You can create a system that allows you to use technology to work smarter and more efficiently. Let's explore how.

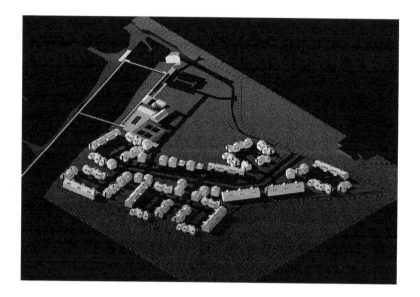

Crisfield, MD—Data in the prototype allows cost and environmental analysis. Parametric data in objects allows unit mix assessment and unit-by-unit sales projections, before designing the units. Links to Google Earth allow assessments in a real-world context.

Process

If you have not integrated your practice, you are living in a world where you could be one of the last holdouts. Every day you see and use products of others who have already gone down this path. Your grocery store is integrated. Your local car care shop is integrated. Your bank is integrated. Integrated processes affect everything you do.

You already have most of the tools to make the change to an integrated practice. Integrated practice requires good business sense. Most of all, it requires good common sense.

> "People need to be reminded more often than they need to be instructed."
> —Dr. Samuel Johnson.

When will you make the change?

You may not have realized how tightly integrated processes are in your world. When you bought your last airplane ticket, did you buy it on the Internet? If so, you interacted with a highly integrated system. Airline ticketing is tightly integrated. You go to a site and type in a few parameters—when, where, and how long— and hit enter. The system searches all available flights to your selected location and gives you the chance to fine-tune your trip. The system quotes the cost, takes your money, and books your flight. Quickly and efficiently.

Behind the scenes, many systems tie together (integrate) to make this happen. You do not see the complexities of systems to track the thousands of planes. You do not see the systems to maintain the engines to keep the aircraft safe. You do not see the personnel tracking system to get the right pilot to the right plane in the right airport at the right time. All you see are the items critical to your current requirement. Thousands of systems integrate to let you book your ticket from the comfort of your home.

Such systems have become so widespread that it makes you question how the built environment fits into this world. What stops architects from embracing the process? What stops them from doing a better job of managing time and costs for their projects?

Rules-based systems

Take a comprehensive look at your processes. Make decisions that, over time, make you more efficient.

Making early, informed decisions and efficiency are hallmarks of an integrated practice. By applying the same tools that your clients use to make informed project decisions, you can better make decisions—about your business.

Is it practical in today's economy to continue to replace drafting by hand with drafting by computer? Does this really improve the quality of your work? Would it be beneficial to use a process that makes what you know more accessible?

At your fingertips, you can have information that is so clear that you can understand the effects of a design decision as it cascades through the environment. Designers of tomorrow will be able to access rich sets of real-time facilities data and will use rules-based systems to eliminate most of the repetitive work. Systems that link business decision-making directly to the design process will be the norm.

These systems exist, although they are not yet in widespread use. You can sign up to use them in your office today. These rules-based systems are rules-of-thumb on steroids. They can codify the knowledge about any subject. By defining how these bits of knowledge interact with each other, they are able to automate most of the fact-based assessments that drive planning.

A simple example:

Extensive lists of everything that makes up a kindergarten classroom exist in many forms. These lists include every desk, chair, pad, toy, chalkboard, light fixture, and toilet. Architects have expertise in the project type. Educators have researched and tested countless approaches to kindergarten.

From this knowledge base, you can define the items that must come together to create a kindergarten classroom. You can create a basic parameters list.

Extensive data exists for the costs of materials and labor, by location codes for much of the world. The same is true for structural loads, accessibility requirements, life safety requirements, and most other codes. Statistics also exist about how many students, teachers, assistants, and parents relate to a given kindergarten classroom.

You can define the measures that control the size, shape and quantities for a kindergarten classroom. You can create metrics.

From these metrics and the parameters list, you can program an intelligent planning system. You can create a system to remove the mundane from the design process.

For example, you can create a system that "knows" that for each five-year-old student, you need x amount of carpet, y amount of general lighting, and z amount of furniture.

A rules-based system for planning kindergarten classrooms starts with a form to allow the user to input the numbers of students and proposed location. From these two inputs, the system computes the size of the space, and the quantities for all parameters that make up the space (floors, walls, ceilings, furniture, systems, equipment, and people). The system also computes all code issues and costs.

By adding intelligent objects that can understand the data created, the system creates a prototype BIM model and places it in Google Earth. The model contains the parametric data for all items that make up the kindergarten classroom, both physical and operational.

This system exists, today.

Decision support

Rules-based systems are a path toward systems that you can use effectively to truly deliver complete BIM for your clients. Onuma Planning System™ (OPS) is online and available today.

The Onuma Planning System is a Web-based application for building owners, designers, contractors, and product manufacturers to help them to manage the full life cycle cost of building ownership. From early planning and schematic design, to design development and automatic construction document output, OPS provides an intuitive user interface that allows you to create complex, shared BIM across a wide section of the industry.

Large-scale facility programs, individual projects and construction product implementations can all use the system. Enterprise clients such as the United States Coast Guard (USCG) use OPS to manage and maintain their facilities and infrastructure systems. They use it to link their facilities to their mission execution. The Coast Guard uses OPS for projects such as their Sector Command Center (SCC) schematic design development process. The result has been improved building life cycle management and better allocation of resources.

The world's largest property manager, the General Services Administration (GSA), lists OPS in their BIM Guide as an approved tool that meets their criteria for an enterprise application to deliver BIM.

Product manufacturers use OPS to manage complex product data in a Web-enabled environment. Manufacturers such as Fypon use OPS to interact with customers on the Web to specify products and automatically generate shop drawings from the OPS database.

You can create complex models with the system, after minimal training. It is not limited to large organizations with training programs. Individuals can effectively use it.

Individual architects, educators and owners use OPS to plan schools, housing and offices. OPS users realize immediate benefits as they create BIMs that automatically connect with other data in distributed systems on the Internet.

Integrated systems, such as OPS, allow users to capture knowledge and better understand how this knowledge connects to the built environment value chain. The system gives the user the ability to analyze information in easy to understand parts, while keeping the information connected to the whole.

You can use the tools in OPS to integrate decision-making with an owner's business processes. By connecting facility information (building condition, available space and physical attributes) with an owner's budgeting, human relations and maintenance planning processes, you make decisions in context. No longer must you make a decision with inaccurate or incomplete data. You make decisions with facts and a clear understanding of relationships.

The ability to make early, informed decisions is one of the major benefits of BIM. Yet, without information sharing and access to data, this benefit never really materializes.

OPS links knowledge across not only one organization but across an entire industry. These links are not apparent at first. Normally these data sources are not interconnected. However, the system is able to exploit information to get the facts and then to serve them up in a form that you can understand and use. As the data sources build, OPS becomes more intelligent. This intelligence allows you to integrate your process with the real world.

Build knowledge with every project

First OPS supported USCG projects.

The data and linkages were then adjusted for GSA BIM Guide requirements.

The system further evolved to support GiS to BIM links to integrate with Google Earth and Open Geospatial Consortium (OGC) standards.

This was an unprecedented feat to develop an open Web service architecture to exchange BIM and GiS data.

The worlds of geographers and architects are converging. Building "blobs" on maps now contain the complete code for everything about the building. They are no longer a geometric shape on a piece of paper. They are BIM. Everything is georeferenced. This convergence has enormous implications for our future as designers and planners of the built environment.

OPS is a Web-based bridge to allow data sharing between both worlds. With this bridge, BIMs can become part of geospatial applications. They can then share information and integrate that information in context. The Web Feature Service (WFS) of OPS uses the linked BIM and GiS data for emergency preparedness and other infrastructure assessment needs. This ability to share and use data across both the building and GiS industries is a model for where integrated practice will go.

You have the ability to integrate BIM and GiS today, using systems such as OPS. Some of the opportunities it offers include:

Automated design

Create a customized system for automating many design processes. Using parameters in a powerful database linked to visual images, you can rapidly assess multiple solutions to complex design problems. Link your institutional knowledge in a Web-service database to support automated design. Capture the knowledge that makes you special.

The combination of automated design with a dashboard view of integrated data allows you to interact and make decisions in real time. A simple, intuitive interface allows you to adjust to changing processes without the need for endless software technical support.

The USCG uses automated design to expedite mission support. Their Sector Command Centers have proven that it is possible to tie design directly to business objectives. These projects use automated processes to generate BIM at the building, space and furniture level from programming requirements input by the user. All while connected to business needs and mission requirements.

Integrated procurement and supply

Create furniture, equipment, and materials in an object database and link them to almost any inventory and procurement program. Existing manufacturer data is also imported and used in the same manner. Suppliers then use this centralized data to allow the automatic shop-drawing generation and other functions. Manufacturers such as Fypon use OPS for this purpose, today.

Automated construction site

The ability of OPS to support open standards and link to distributed systems through Web services allows multiple solutions for intelligent and automated construction sites.

Intelligent facility operations

Predict when and where to expend resources to best support mission requirements using facility condition information and mission dependency measures.

Lifecycle management and information integration

By capturing knowledge and storing it in OPS, you retain corporate knowledge. You provide new staff with dependable historical data that would otherwise be lost as experienced staff retire or move to other opportunities.

An intuitive user interface allows your staff to teach themselves how to use the system. As they interact with the tools, the system adapts assisting in life cycle data management. This is one of the highest forms of information integration.

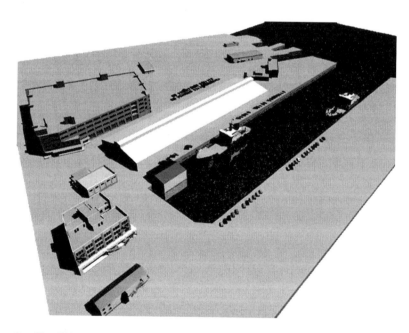

Seattle, WA—As-built facility model. Multi-facility complexes are ideal candidates for BIM. By archiving actual conditions, owners can better assess how their facilities affect missions and business processes. Over time, such models form the basis for fully integrated BIM.

CHAPTER 5

Seven steps guide your way

Pioneers such as Kimon Onuma are producing systems that allow you to work and use rules-based systems in the BIM environment, today. As more of these systems roll out and mature, you will be able to do things that were once only dreams. In order to get the maximum benefit from these tools, focus on changing your business in the following ways:

1. Be self-aware—know and really understand how you work.

2. Embrace the philosophy of "fail-fast." Move on rather than continuing flawed processes.

3. Engage others earlier in a more collaborative ways.

4. Maximize knowledge and productivity in the front end of projects.

5. Adjust fee structures.

6. Manage liabilities.

7. Improve your bottom line by improving productivity.

These steps define a practice philosophy that enables integrated practice. hNext, we will look at each step in detail.

1. Self-awareness

Knowing yourself and understanding how your business delivers services is the first step to successful integrated practice.

First, understand your design process.

Traditionally, planning, design, construction, and facility management were entirely separate tasks in the life cycle of a building. From the perspective of the building owner, separating these tasks often resulted in additional costs and inefficiencies.

The fact that you are reading this book likely means that you have realized that it is virtually impossible to catch up to the trends, unless you develop a new practice paradigm.

Over the last century, architects began to focus on the design phase, with some overlap into the other areas. This focus created a very cyclic business process. Working in what is now an antiquated design process, architects are rapidly losing their role as leaders of the built environment. Owners are demanding that architects improve how they design and manage projects, now.

To implement BIM methodology truly means understanding your own design process. Much recent discussion about building information modeling centers on architects' resistance to change. Some see architects as a major factor in keeping these benefits from building owners. Architects are, in many venues, seen as a major impediment to successful deployment and implementation of BIM.

Integrating technology into the design business requires learning to manage change. How you approach staffing, clients, and consultants changes to coordinate with BIM processes and an information-centric world. Implementation requires changes to business and design processes, a commitment to embracing new technologies and a high level of responsibility.

Create a new way to do business. Realize how interconnected you are with others. Make yourself a leader in providing value in this new world. Expand your vision of the world—and your vision of where you fit in the building industry. Move to a process designed for today—and tomorrow.

How you work

First, look at how you set up projects and how you generate design solutions. Understand your skills and deficiencies—your strengths and weaknesses.

Begin by questioning everything and digging into the processes used by others. Break everything down into its smallest components. From these components, you will create processes that really work for you. You will tailor your firm to capitalize on your strengths and to overcome your weaknesses.

We find that Mindjet's mind mapping software is the ideal medium for documenting and communication this type of process. With MindManager, you process snippets of data about yourself. You organize them to find patterns. You brainstorm and see where your thoughts take you while keeping track and building a map of how you work.

By understanding how you work, you build a framework for integrating technology—in ways that work best for you. By tailoring your processes, you deliver the benefits available from today's best tools and high-performance processes, today.

Manage constraints

There are many constraints on how you do the business of design. By identifying and correctly managing constraints, you can manage the performance of any complex process.

As we began our explorations, we found ourselves studying the Theory of Constraints (TOC). In 1984, physicist turned business consultant, Dr. Eliyahu Goldratt published *The Goal*. He theorized that any business could improve its bottom line results through applying scientific methods to resolving organizational problems. Goldratt theorized that each business has a single constraint that limits its performance relative to its goal. By managing this constraint, you can overcome obstacles to production and become more efficient and responsive.

TOC looks at an organization as a system rather than as a hierarchy. Goldratt's theory explains why agency construction management works. It is also a major driver behind Toyota's phenomenal success in recent years. TOC underpins many of the management approaches that work best today.

Studying the theory and its applications, you will find that either you can manage constraints or they will manage you. Deciding how to manage these constraints is critical to your success.

Understand that if you try to manage everything, you are not really managing anything.

This leads to many questions:

- How do you decide what to manage?

- Can you improve how you manage projects and how you develop design solutions?

- If you constrain the process, will it affect the quality of the final design?

- What constraint(s) can you use to manage the process more effectively?

Architects who are not managing constraints create much of the poor documentation, cost overruns, and other problems cited by owners in recent years. By not managing constraints, they enable many of the problems. Even with normal project management controls.

Adaptive reuse, Annapolis, MD, 1994. Adaptive reuse project designed and constructed using management of cost constraints and virtual building models.

You can control the design and construction process by managing constraints. It is a four-step process:

- The first step in applying TOC is to identify the constraints on your process.

- The second step involves deciding how you will use the constraint to improve performance toward your goal.

- The third is to make the constraint important—give it power by integrating it into your process.

- The final step is to make the constraint less of a constraint by making it part of your everyday work process.

In our explorations, we identified that **COSTS** in all its forms, is the primary constraint on architectural processes today. We have come to believe that management of cost constraints is the single most important change that you can make to improve how you support your clients.

Manage cost constraints throughout your process. By managing cost constraints your outcomes will improve in positive and owner-centered ways. Managing cost as a constraint has worked for over twenty years! Ask any successful agency construction manager.

2. Fail fast and move on

The world is changing every day. Daily you see new technologies, new ideas, and new ways of doing things. These changes make things happen faster. They put you into direct contact with many more people. They remove the things that divide us from the world.

Some of these changes are good. Some are bad. Most simply add to the complexity. In this environment, you must be a lifelong learner. Constantly explore and evaluate new technologies and new methods to improve your business.

As a rule, people assume that any new technology should be thoroughly tested and proven before they adopt it. However, this is not always true in today's rapidly changing world. Today you should explore as many options as possible as quickly as possible. You are searching for the optimum tools and approach to do the best job on each assignment. As you explore, try new things and discard those that do not work.

When you fully test every tool, you may find yourself constantly behind the curve. It is better to create a system that allows you to assess a new tool quickly. If it works, consider the tool for deployment. If not, quickly move on to the next possibility.

You need to make the best and most effective use of your time in this environment. That does not mean that you can push everything off to subordinates. An integrated process requires active and continuous involvement from your most qualified people. You can delegate some of these tasks, and not others.

Develop a solid understanding and the ability to function in any of the core tools that your firm uses.

You do not have to be expert in all parts of any tool. Building detail into models, adding data, and producing bidding documents are all tasks that you can assign to others. Rapid conceptualizing is much harder to assign. This is where the ability to synthesize is critical and experience counts. For this, the designer must use the tools.

This book refrains from making recommendations about which bim modeling tool is best for you. This is for several reasons.

First and foremost, your modeling tool is a highly personal decision. Become comfortable in creating in whichever tool you choose. Early decision-making requires that you create usable data early in the process.

To get many of the benefits that integrated practice offers, become fluent in using these tools for conceptualization and design.

There are obviously examples of senior designers who have others create models for them. For most firms, this approach dilutes the value and benefits for the firm and their clients. Others will argue differently. However, you should learn how to do this with your very own hands, mind, and computer.

Today, too many senior architects talk a good game and hope that their staff can figure it out well enough to keep their clients happy. Take the time and learn the tools that will let you conceptualize your designs.

Testing

Ignore the hype and forget the marketing. Put your preconceptions aside. In this area, brand name recognition means little. Any of the vendors that sell Industry Foundation Class (IFC) certified products can sell you a bim solution. Vendors develop all types of strategies for getting architects to purchase their products. You see everything from giving away updates to non-BIM legacy products to subscription services. None of these really matter to your decision. If the software does not improve your process and if you are not comfortable in working with it, you should not buy it.

The costs of bim software products pale in comparison to the costs of a twelve-month trial that turns out to be a mistake. Such a trial can be an excruciating experience. Many firms that have tried to implement bim tools based entirely on their legacy systems have seen suboptimal results. In fact, depending on how you define the term, many of them have failed.

Find the product that lets you do work, as easily and effectively as possible.

Finding the right product may take some trial and error. Nevertheless, this search can happen quickly. The following approach to testing new products has worked for others:

Set aside three days to try a major new product.

The first day, go through the product tutorial, step by step. Alternately, sign up for the vendor's one-day introduction course. This is the computer equivalent of "reading the book."

The second day, begin a new project. It should be a project that is typical for your firm, whether a new facility or a renovation. This should be something real, not something from the tutorial. Do not select the project for simplicity. You want to make this a real-life test.

By the end of the third day, your model should include—floors, walls, roofs, doors, windows, stairs, toilet and kitchen fixtures, and a basic ground plane. As a minimum, you should have produced photo-rendered images, presentation-grade plans, and elevations. All of these images should be at a quality level that is good enough to present to clients, with no apologies.

You should have also extracted the areas for all spaces with quantities and areas of doors, windows, and wall and roof surfaces. Some architects have also produced a virtual reality model or tested their model in online systems such as "Green Building Studio" at this point.

You have created your first prototype. You have had a productive three-day exercise that should be billable. If you are comfortable with the product, you may have found your modeling tool. If you cannot achieve at least this level of product by the end of the third day, try another modeling tool.

By the end of your three-day test you should have created a model similar to this. Or better!

3. Engage others

You work with many different people now. Do you sometimes feel a little like the conductor of an orchestra, coordinating consultants, staff, contractors, and a host of others to get projects completed? Is it even possible to be more collaborative?

One of the major requirements for integrated practice are skills called—"knowing and using your resources" and "understanding the group."

Get a handle on what everyone has to offer. This is what social networking and relationship management are all about. You are a member of networks that can in one way or another help the overall team. Each of us has a group of colleagues that we can depend on to do a good job in a pinch. You know how to charge for their time, know when they might be interested and know how to work with them. Integrated practice lets you bring them even closer. It lets you expand the value of your network.

Communication ensures that you and your network are effective in delivering value. In an integrated practice environment, your attitude is that it is not possible for any of the team to succeed if one of the team has failed.

> I hope that teamwork is the basis on which your network operates. By working to find common objectives, sharing information and developing open and honest business standards, you can be a leader in the process.

Encourage everyone to realize his or her full potential to develop creative ideas. By engaging others and focusing on the long view, the leadership opportunities grow exponentially. Successfully moving to an integrated practice means that you engage your staff, consultants, vendors and clients in the process. If you lead the way, they will come to understand and buy into your vision. They will learn to take the long view and together you will be successful.

4. Maximize front end

Understand that you work in a world of highly interconnected processes. Because of these interconnections, you have the ability to impact things far in the future. You can change things in ways that increase the chance of future success. You can create processes that minimize future problems. Alternatively, you can continue to design in a partial vacuum that leaves owners bearing the costs.

> Frank Lloyd Wright said, "Man built most nobly when limitations were at their greatest."

Letting constraints manage you, rather than being proactive, drives poor documentation, cost overruns, and late delivery. Put aside your fears and concerns. Embrace the broader issues. Use technology to improve outcomes for your projects. Provide better value.

There are many constraints in any architectural process. If you try to manage them all, you probably will end up not managing much of anything. Using concepts from the Theory of Constraints, you will find that if you manage costs, you can control the downstream process, in a positive and owner-centered way.

You have likely used Cost of Change curves to explain how changes made late in projects result in much greater costs than changes made early. It is obviously much more expensive to change after pouring the concrete than when the architect is first conceiving the project.

For architects, the greatest benefits from integrated practice come from tweaking the design and production process to take advantage of the Cost of Change curves.

Traditional process fees

To illustrate the problem, let us consider a hypothetical process. The process goes something like this:

1. You review the owner's program and develop a concept. You quote a cost per square foot that is no more accurate than the budget the owner developed in the program. The

Schematic Design phase uses between 10% and 15% of your fee.

2. You then develop the concept to define the systems. With a well-managed process, you build on the first step. You refine the concept and your engineers create system concepts. You refine the cost-per-square-foot estimate. Design Development uses 15% to 20% of your fee.

3. You then produce construction documents. With a smooth process, you build upon the first two steps. More often than not, here is where you and the owner make most of the detailed decisions for the project. Sometimes the decisions require major changes to the work completed in the first steps. Near the end of this process, you prepare your first estimate based on unit costs and assemblies. Construction Documents use 30-45% of your fee.

4. You then package the documents and bid the work to contractors. Since there has been little (if any) interaction with contractors prior to this, you issue the work and then hold an office betting pool to see who guesses the closest. Procurement uses about 5% of your fee.

5. Finally, you receive bids. The chips fall where they may. They could be high—they could be low. Common wisdom suggests that they are usually high. If the bids are high, you work with the contractor to cut things out to get to budget—you re-engineer but do not get much value in return. You redesign to cut things out—usually without additional fees. You then have 15-25% of your fee to administer the problems caused by these after-the-fact changes.

What is wrong with this scenario?

The owner paid the architect three-fourths of his or her fee before the problem occurred. The owner bears the costs of the items value-engineered out after bidding or other problems that develop.

The owner wonders why the architect was not smart enough to see it coming. From the perspective of integrated practice and best use of the Cost-of-Change curve—everything is wrong!

Later in the book, we look at how you can change this process, in detail, but for now an overview:

Use BIM and your knowledge base at the beginning of projects. Make every possible decision, as early in the process as possible. Conceive the design using building information models from the beginning of the process.

Manage costs, because now you can get reliable quantities early and often. Use your building information models to communicate with constructors and suppliers early in the process. Tailor procurement to owner requirements and to the most efficient delivery process, for your location.

Your fee allocations change. The owner has more certainty of outcomes before spending most of the design fee.

Now let us look at an integrated approach to the same scenario. We will look at how your fees change when you work in an integrated process.

5. Fees change

As a young architect, I was taught that you had to match the work effort to the available fees, if you hoped to be profitable. When the costs to deliver a project exceed the fee for the project, you are in big trouble.

Architects sometimes forget this simple equation, because they are architects first and business people second. They sometimes value the design process much more highly than others do.

Architects sometimes work their way into traps that get them into trouble.

- They spend excessive time refining the design.

- They undercut their ability to do the detailing and construction documents.

- They focus on the aesthetics and forget to answer the mundane questions of how and how much.

- They delude themselves into believing that they understand what drives the owner and what makes construction efficient.

The traditional five-phased process minimizes architects' abilities. The process is fraught with disconnected tasks, repetitive work and mundane processes. In theory, the process moves from gateway to gateway, building detail as you progress. In reality, it is inefficient and unwieldy.

If you step back, look at the character traits of a good architect, and compare them to the character traits that would get the most from the traditional process—there are major misalignments. The traditional process is much like an assembly line—getting high volume from a large contingent of semi-skilled laborers.

Integrated practice is a very different approach.

- It more closely aligns with the characteristics that we associate with architects.

- It reduces or eliminates mundane and repetitive input.

- It works best for those that can synthesize complex data.

- It reduces the workflow problems that currently plague architect's offices.

- It makes it possible for creative designers to focus on design, supported transparently by knowledge captured in the tools.

In the last chapter, we looked at how you allocate fees in the traditional process. You allocate your fees differently in an integrated process. In both you estimate the actual work effort on each project and allocate the fees based on the work effort. In an integrated process, you focus much more attention on the earliest steps in the design process.

Adjust your fee percentages to match the work effort. This makes the fees heavier on the front end.

Overall integrated project fees have proven to be less than or equal to the "normal" fees. They front-load, however.

Experience has shown that owners highly value processes that front-load decision-making. These processes make owners more confident and certain about where their project is heading.

By structuring your process to take advantage of this perceived value, you have the opportunity to create additional services. As a minimum, you have the opportunity to focus the project's direction. You also have the opportunity to ensure that you are basing your services on the most accurate scope and project scale.

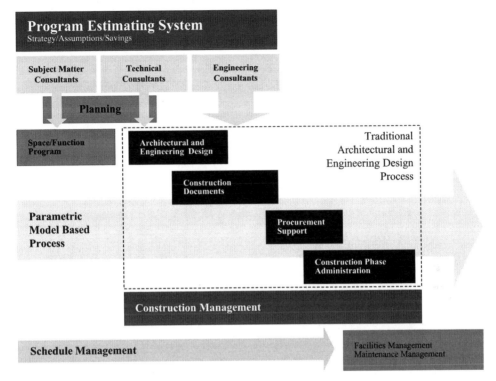

Integrated practice and BIM focus on just-in-time decision-making to improve predictability and give clients more assurance of outcomes.

Integrated process fees

To illustrate the fee structure that you may encounter, consider another hypothetical process. The process goes something like this:

1. You develop a validation study. Within the study, you analyze needs and objectives and create prototype models. You prepare a master schedule and project strategy. You prepare cost models, cost assumptions and comparisons. You run solar, sustainability, and other analyses. Then you spend the time to review all of this with the owner. You document the decisions and embed them in your prototype. Validation uses 20-25% of your fee.

2. You add detail to the validated prototype. Alternatively, start a new prototype from scratch using the validation as the design control. From this model, you are able to extract nearly any graphic that you can envision. You embed consultant data. You extract views to create bridged design/build bidding documents or prepare for a more detailed model in the next step. You refine costs and analyses. The concept prototype process uses 20-25% of your fee.

3. Assuming that construction is procured through public bid general contractors, you add more detail to the concept prototype to extract construction documents. The bulk of work on this model involves composing sheets, cleaning up sections, and conducting quality assurance operations. You refine costs and analyses. The construction prototype uses 25% of your fee.

4. You then package the documents and bid the work to contractors. Since you have shared the documents with constructors and the owner from the beginning, you have a clear idea where you are going. You focus on responding to all questions and concerns—you let nothing drop through the cracks. Your goal is to eliminate all uncertainty at the bid table. Procurement uses about 8% of your fee.

5. Finally, you receive bids. You are still at the mercy of the market. However, you have now analyzed, tested, and verified to a level where you have eliminated confusion and the need for most contingencies. Experience has shown that the bids will be within 5% of the budget you validated in the first step. You now have 17-27% of your fee to administer a clear and well-understood project.

The process moves decisions to the beginning. It focuses your energies on creating the correct solution and allocates the funds to support your efforts. The process gives the owner a high degree of certainty. It retains at least as much fee in the construction process as in the traditional process.

You focus your creative energies on getting quality decisions early. You minimize downstream problems. You become more focused on the design and less focused on production. The tools automate much of that for you. Freeing you up to do what you do best.

Design and solve problems.

6. Manage liability

In the perfect world of the future, architects will be able to design and problem-solve without a care in the world. Architects and builders will not argue. Lawsuits will be outdated. Everyone will work in perfect harmony, sharing data with no concern for intellectual property rights. Nothing is wasted.

Yes, right! It is probably not going to happen.

The reality is that you have to work in an environment where traditional delivery processes, your software systems and your approach to contracts all contribute to distrust and adversarial relationships. Architects have to watch what they do all the time. Each project phase is independent of those that precede and follow. Everyone focuses on avoiding risks.

There are risks in any new process.

If you are going to avoid them, approach integrated design and BIM with open eyes. The construction industry is changing, like it

Harold Wilson, a British prime minister said, "He who rejects change is the architect of decay. The only human institution which rejects progress is the cemetery."

or not. You can either proactively change with it, or you can find something else to do.

You are likely already wrestling with this change. Otherwise why read this book? Figuring out how to protect your assets, your good name and your family, are important considerations as you move forward.

Some of the questions that need answers include:

- Does my professional liability insurance cover the potential risks and exposures from this change? Do standardized agreements address the exposure from this change?

- Will integrated practice alter the standard of care that we are responsible to provide?

- When we embed incorrect data in the model, what happens? Who is responsible for incorrect information and how is risk assigned when it is unclear who created the data (or who created the problem)?

- How can I share the risks equitably across the entire project team (including the owner)?

- What information do all team members share to deliver on their responsibilities?

- What exposure will I have when I front-load information and decision-making?

The biggest benefit from traditional processes may be that there are precedents. You know how to react since most problems have happened before. You also know that, when somebody makes a claim, your insurance carrier and attorney will know how to react. Since the system is in place, you can continue to work as usual and let someone else handle the problems.

Unfortunately, there are major problems with business as usual.

By continuing as usual, you will continue to have problems. Only by proactively changing, do you have a chance to move your firm to a better place.

Paraphrasing Albert Einstein—"Insanity is doing the same thing over and over again and expecting different results."

The world is moving away from a hierarchal—*command and control model* to a distributed—*share and collaborate model.* A model that values processes and systems that improve information flow and creates a more sustainable environment.

This change is happening everywhere, not only in the construction industry. To work effectively in this new model, move away from focusing on the WE—THEY and start looking out for US.

Look to the traditional process as an example:

You now give control of your documents to low-bidding contractors in a public forum. Some of these contractors have business plans that exploit any error, omission, or ambiguity. Since the documents are by necessity never perfect, the flaws create additional costs and other problems. The owner gets upset. It is the classic WE—THEY situation. You are at risk.

Whether you recognize it as such, you have made a business decision to rely on insurance to protect your interests.

You have other options. You can make a conscious business decision to take on the responsibility for making better outcomes happen. You can understand where the process creates bottlenecks and conflicts. You can develop strategies to mitigate risks. You still have to have insurance, but now you become proactive.

This decision is fundamental to delivering superior performance through integrated practice.

Three-quarters of all respondents in the *2007 Value from VDC / BIM* Use survey conducted by John Kunz and Brian Gilligan of the Center for Integrated Facility Engineering (CIFE) at Stanford University said that "virtual design and construction reduces risk."

The integrated practice business model is bound to generate new risks. By proactively managing these risks, you become a valuable commodity. Your focus moves away from fear and risk avoidance to risk management and risk sharing.

Managing risks and sharing them equitably requires you to understand the knotty issues that surround risk management.

- It requires you to develop relationships with a circle of trusted advisors who are willing to help you make informed decisions. You have to be closer than ever to your insurance carrier and your attorneys.

- It requires you to develop a process for actively communicating about risk with your consultants, constructors and clients.

- It requires you to manage owner and contractor expectations. Create a building information modeling process designed to manage expectations of perfection.

When you couple your resources with a well-thought-out delivery process, taking on the additional responsibility becomes less of a problem.

Your models allow greater consistency and compliance with standards. They make it easier to find and resolve conflicts. By solving problems on the spot, you help to keep the job moving and reduce the risk of suits or claims from design errors and omissions. By finding problems quickly, you reduce the unintended consequences that can occur.

By working more collaboratively, you make changes that reduce surprises during bidding and construction. You improve the project, reduce costly change orders, and delay claims.

Experience has shown that when you take responsibility and control, you have less risk.

Work toward a shared approach to risk management across the entire delivery team. Owners, constructors, consultants and suppliers should understand the issues. When we reach a point where risks are shared based on equitable allocations that recognize the level of effort and the rewards, this will be much less of an issue.

Because of the current state of the industry, take leadership on this issue. Be proactive. When owners know that you are working to solve their problems everything seems to go better. A proactive approach to managing risks is likely the best solution in the short run.

As integrated processes become universal, many of the issues will be resolved. Someday, there will be precedents for how to react to problems in this environment. Realize that this is an evolving issue, keep on top of the changes and make course corrections to manage the risks.

Keep in mind that, in an integrated practice, you cannot allow software to replace professional judgment.

If you allow captured knowledge and rules-based planning to "take control," you are ceding responsibility and leaving yourself open to problems. This is one of the reasons that it is important for experienced designers to become more involved in the process. In an integrated process, knowledgeable designers must develop the sketch from the back of the napkin—do not hand it off to inexperienced staff.

Pay attention to the details, from beginning to end.

Lao Tse said it best in the sixth century BC—"Men in business affairs come near perfection, then fail. If they were as attentive at the end as at the beginning, their business would succeed."

7. Improve productivity

The majority of architects work in small firms.

The American Institute of Architects in its 2006 Firm Survey Report, found that 58.3% of total architects' staff worked in firms with fewer than fifty employees.

Yet, the focus of most of the attention on BIM and integrated practice is on the largest firms. Because of this, many smaller firms question the value of the integrated process. The process seems far removed from today's small practices. It is an attractive idea, but for many small firms it is hard to see profitable applications today. If you believe the hype, it seems as though it works only for large, high-value projects. Nothing could be further from the truth.

Integrated practice offers benefits for firms of all shapes and sizes.

The trick is to tailor the process to your firm. Do not depend on any "one-size-fits-all" approach. Do not depend on integrating everything at once. You do not have to integrate with construction or operations and maintenance to provide benefits to owners. You do not have to wait until someone else works everything out.

Large firms may have the workforce and financial resources to integrate everything. They may have the prestige to convince multinational software developers to use them as "test-sites." You probably do not have the same backing.

That should not keep you from doing the things that you can do now. It does not keep you from using the technology and improved processes to be more profitable or keep you from doing a better job for your clients.

There are several other interesting statistics in the AIA survey. Did you know that most architects consider planning, predesign, and construction to be the least profitable parts of their businesses? Did you know that non-architectural design services are rare in the business?

Moreover, basic design services are the most profitable. Does your firm fit this profile? If so, integrated practice offers many opportunities for you to improve your bottom line. You can think of this as a process that makes early phases profitable and improves your construction phase results.

It lets you focus on design.

Reading to this point, you have likely started to get a feeling for why BIM and integrated practice will improve your process. When owners understand the value of integrated practice, it becomes a marketable and profitable addition to your repertoire. Planning and predesign are where integrated processes offer immediate results. Using bim tools and changing your process workflow is the foundation for everything else.

One-step at a time is usually the best way to integrate your practice.

It is possible, now

The relationship between Toyota and Ford Motors is a metaphor for the changes that are now influencing the companies that affect the built environment. Ford, founded in 1903, created the standard for volume production using unskilled laborers. After WWII, Toyota was a cheap import, for the young with no money.

Move forward to 2007 and Toyota is number one in the automobile industry. Ford Motors is resizing, dropping unprofitable and inefficient models, shutting down facilities, and consolidating production lines.

Toyota first surpassed Ford's revenues in 2004. They set the worldwide standard and license their hybrid technology to other auto manufacturers. Consumers perceive that Toyota delivers better value in terms of fuel economy, reliability, and quality.

What changed?

The Toyota Production System (TPS) has driven Toyota to become the world's leading automaker. TPS is in the DNA of everything at Toyota. It embeds an organizational belief system that strives to get things done perfectly, the first time. Consumers drive TPS. It focuses on minimizing waste and continually improves processes. TPS builds long-term relationships. Most of all, it is flexible and quick to react. TPS integrates dealing fairly with everyone with well-informed use of technology. Toyota Motors used these concepts to create integrated processes that changed concepts of manufacturing.

Today you can enter the model, color, and accessory choices for a new Toyota; close financing; start your new car into production and arrange for delivery—all from your wireless laptop in the comfort of your home lounge chair.

We do the same thing when we buy computers. Soon we will do it for many more products—perhaps even buildings.

Alvin Toffler was the first to popularize the concepts of "mass customization" and "just-in-time production."

You need to understand the theory and drivers behind today's successful processes. Without this background information, you may find yourself "reinventing the wheel." You could also invest a lot of time, only to find out too late that you are repeating unsuccessful processes.

Ask questions. Why is Toyota so successful? Why is Ford on the ropes? Step back and look at how Toyota's process works:

- It is best to begin by looking at what makes their process so special. Start with a solid understanding of the theories.

- Understand why TPS works while architects' processes seem to be lagging. Understand the underlying reasons why their process works. What makes it tick?

- Explore the best ways to integrate their ideas into your process.

- Understand how Toyota achieved integrated ordering, production, and delivery. The process includes many parallels that can improve your business.

The Toyota Production System should give you many ideas. Many of the concepts are directly applicable. The greatest lesson from TPS is not in the individual parts, but in the whole of the process. TPS works because it permeates everything at Toyota, from top to bottom.

This is the example to take away.

You can integrate architectural practice with a strategy driven by owners, your staff, and proven business theory.

The process should not be "process reengineering." It should not be a radical redesign or require a "clean slate" that disregards the status quo.

You start with an honest clear view of where you are now and chart the changes that will move you toward your goal of an integrated practice.

Values drive the change

The concepts that drive Toyota's system apply directly to the systems and processes of the built environment. The TPS system includes these basic values:

- Take the long view; even if it affects short-term gains.

- Minimize waste at all levels—people, production, and resources. Eliminate wasted effort.

- Maximize efficiency, even at low volume.

- Produce many different products quickly and efficiently.

- Make quality the first priority.

- Empower people. Use consensus and rapid decision-making.

- Place value on organization and control.

- Use technology to serve people and processes.

- Educate leaders. Become lifelong learners.

- Team success is the measure of success.

- Share risks, costs and information.

- Make decisions based on proven results.

The lesson to learn from TPS is that many small steps correctly focused will make a major impact. Everyone shares in outcomes and anyone can stop the process to correct problems.

Using many small things done properly and consistently to achieve big results is what integrated practice is all about.

Integrated practice values

Toyota's TPS relies on a series of values to guide their company. Successful integrated practice also begins with values. Without an agreed upon set of values, it becomes difficult to stay the course. The tendency is to wander off-track or to revert to the comfortable way of doing things when there is no clearly annunciated set of values. A system of values gives a framework from which to make daily decisions. The values that drive integrated practice are:

- Be flexible and adapt to change. Plan and design for the life cycle of the asset. Take the long view.
- Define success at the beginning and set appropriate expectations.
- Solve problems as early as possible in the process. Early decisions have a major impact on the final product (and they cost the least).
- Remove subjectivity. Get a good, objective definition of quality.
- Keep the owner involved.
- Understand the underlying need. LISTEN—communicate openly to understand expectations.
- Form partnerships with people you trust. Avoid competition—work together.
- Take responsibility and make things happen.

The example set by the Toyota Production System shows the value and importance of an easily understood system that everyone in the firm can embrace. Use this list to begin the value list for your firm. Develop the list with input from everyone. When it begins to take hold, post it for all to see.

Perceptions

Architects have the training and skills to be successful in this environment. In fact, architects are uniquely qualified to lead the process. They can help to build a world where the watchwords are thrift and sustainability. They can become leaders in anticipating and creating a better tomorrow.

Not everyone will agree with this assessment. Not everyone can look to the future and move-on from the past. Your strategy should consider this.

Planning begins with exploration and self-knowledge.

Put this change into a context that you can understand. Without an understanding of the context and issues that affect you, it is difficult to plan for solutions. Explore the questions and concerns of those you affect in the design and construction process. Begin to see patterns. Handle the issues that affect your practice.

These comments are a small subset of people's perception of architects. They do however offer an interesting perspective. Do you see a pattern? What can architects do to change these perceptions?

Begin the Change

Certainly, these comments do not reflect on many of the good things that architects provide. However, they are examples of some of the issues and concerns that clients are willing to share. You can correct these issues for your clients and their projects. You can do a better job and deliver better value.

By effectively using the best available technology, processes, and tools, you will find solutions that work for you and your

Over a recent six-month period, we recorded comments from people who have experience with architects. We wanted to understand how they think about architects. We were looking for perceptions and impressions.

The comments that we received from this process are interesting and a little scary. Although this was not a scientific study, the comments offer an interesting perspective on the issues. Here are the responses we received, by category:

Cost

Architects' estimates are at best suspect or "just plain wrong."

Poorly coordinated documents are creating problems and costing me money.

Bids significantly over budget are the rule—not the exception.

Architects do not really care about costs.

Time

Using an architect will make the project take too long.

The contractor will make sure that the architect performs.

Management

Can architects really work in an integrated process?

Architects do not understand the "real world."

The architect's process is not open—"what the heck" are they doing for me?

Architects do not manage risks well. They push everything off on others.

Architects think that they can do everything—well, they really can't.

Architects believe that the construction industry revolves around them, but it doesn't, not by a long shot.

Leadership

Architects sell high ethics and then don't take responsibility.

There always seems to be a lot of conflict between the architect and others.

Technology

I don't care how you do it.

Mechanical systems are where we have the long-term issues.

Every architect I talk to shows me computer images. Why should I care? You can all do it.

clients. It does not matter if you are a sole practitioner or part of a large firm—integrated practice makes it easier to solve the problems described above. Otherwise, what are you integrating?

Reading this far, you know that you are starting an organizational change process. You know how to begin to apply integrated practices to your firm.

First, look at overarching concepts that work.

Then look at systematic processes that you can apply on projects every day.

Next, we discuss how integrated practice works day-to-day.

Plan for tomorrow

At the bleeding edge, few players actually know what they are doing. Even they use a lot of trial and error. Many people in all segments of the construction industry are involved. Many of them are focusing on standards and the future. They are doing high cost "test cases." They spend a lot of time in committees preparing standards that contain jargon that few can understand. They are debating the minutia of data exchanges.

The focus that others are taking on standards and interoperability is necessary and great for the future, but it does not help you to do real work today.

Without clean, affordable and dependable ways to manage and exchange the information that you are developing with bim models, you may not see long-term returns on your investment. Without standards, bim is a more effective delivery system day-to-day, but it does not produce ongoing income. With standards, BIM opens up a completely new world of residual income possibilities. The data in your models becomes valuable long after you design and construct the project.

Consider this in your long-term plans.

About twelve years ago, we realized that we could not sell BIM. Not a single client had a clue about BIM. No one was willing to pay for it. We realized that we had to do something different.

Beyond that, BIM did not really describe what we were doing. Our goal was to create and use an information archive through the lifecycle of the built environment. We planned to use this archive to level the cyclical nature of the design business. We believed that it would generate opportunities for residual income streams.

To most people, BIM did not clearly describe much of anything. It certainly did not describe how architects should work in today's world.

That is why we started to use the term—BEYOND INFORMATION MODELS. It seemed to describe what we were really doing. The information models were only a part of the equation.

What really got the results were all the things that revolve around the models. Clients were willing to pay us to get their projects done better. They were not willing to invest in a database that might (or might not) have value some day.

Beyond Information Models has become synonymous with using technology to improve processes to relieve clients' stress. You help them get certainty about their projects.

You can actually explain this to clients. It is easy for them to understand that they benefit if you use technology to get them more and better decision-making information, earlier in the process.

Clients see value in certainty. They understand it and are willing to pay for it.

When you think about it, who can better manage the range of variables and complexity that affect your clients' projects? You can!

This is where you can create better design and become more valuable to your clients.

PART III

THE PROCESS
DAY TO DAY

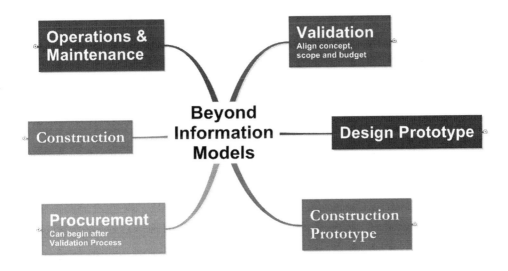

Operations &
Maintenance

Validation
Align concept,
scope and budget

Construction

Beyond
Information
Models

Design Prototype

Procurement
Can begin after
Validation Process

Construction
Prototype

CHAPTER 6

Certainty is your mantra

 BY CREATING AND MANAGING building models, you are using a process that defines how architectural projects ought to happen. Your process requires defined working practices, methodologies, and behaviors. Your process overlays multi-stage prototyping and parametric cost management on the traditional five-phase process immortalized in American Institute of Architect's contract documents.

At Design Atlantic Ltd, we call our process 4SiteSystems. It takes advantage of data extracted from the virtual building model to better program and anticipate design solutions. The process places emphasis on early project decisions.

The 4SiteSystems process starts with a Validation Phase, which forms the foundation for all further efforts. By applying the process, we have achieved improvements in our productivity and profitability. In addition, we have significantly improved outcomes for our clients.

We have seen our ability to "predict" bid results improve using the process. Beginning in 2001, we have seen consistent project savings of about 10%.

By example, we used the process to public bid design/build at the Salisbury Fire Headquarters and Station 16 project (included in the Case Studies later in this book). This project received three responsive public bids. The Program Estimate from the Validation Phase was 0.6% above the low bid and contract award. Costs throughout the construction process have closely tracked the Program Estimate.

You might dismiss examples like this as flukes. Nevertheless, we have consistently seen this level of result for over six years.

The integrated 3D building prototypes created during the process enable an owner to make decisions about costs early in the process, thereby significantly improving their ability to accurately budget. The rich set of building data created during the design and documentation phase of the project remains relevant even after the building is constructed.

The benefits come from consistently applying and reinforcing the concepts that anchor the process. We use the best available tools for the job at hand. Yet the tools (applications) are secondary. The goal is an improved project with positive outcomes, every time.

Focus on providing sustained value for your clients. Eliminate or reduce inefficiencies in the process. Eliminate repetitive and mundane tasks.

By doing this you become the steward of your client's resources. Your process creates an archive of information in interoperable databases. You use this data to help your clients maintain and operate the facility—allowing others to benefit from it for many years to come.

Basic Concepts

Architects have limited themselves to a small part of the built environment. They have boxed themselves in to a small piece of the action because of real and imaginary issues and perceptions of risks.

Architects typically focus on designing buildings. That is one of the things that they are trained to do. That is what they have insurance to cover. Yet, the narrow definition of this context limits their ability to embrace new possibilities. Because of it, their influence is limited to a very small segment of the construction world. Architects have boxed themselves into a small corner of the built environment.

Obviously, some architects work in a bigger context. However, attitudes and the general perception tend to place artificial limits on their ability to apply their skills in the wider venue. There are opportunities out there in many other areas.

Architects have unique skills. They can thrive in an information-centered world. This requires a focus on the "big picture" with a clear understanding of what creates value.

Step back and look at the "first principles" that drive your practice. The key is to find the important changes that can expand what you do and have the greatest impact. Analyze the thinking of those who came before. Evaluate successful management systems in parallel industries. Map your internal processes and procedures. All with the goal of understanding what architects really do (or could do) in today's world.

This exploration and the desire to leverage the best available technologies led us to create 4SiteSystems. In early 1997, we formalized the process with the goal of overcoming the shortfalls of doing architecture the "old-fashioned way." In broad terms, we conceived the system to revolve around eight basic concepts. The concepts affect how you look at projects and how you deliver services.

The concepts that drive 4SiteSystems include:

1. Early decisions. Take a predesign decision-making focus. Embrace dependable decision-making information. Use technology to get owners a high level of quality information at the right time in the process.

2. A long view. Use a systems approach to design. Understand that this is a process and you can define and manage any process.

3. Management of constraints. Understand that you can manage complex processes by constraints. Cost is the main constraint that we use to manage the process.

4. Cultural competency. Embrace free and open communications. Know that people work better and make better decisions when they are informed about what is happening. Embrace processes that bring all points of view and all skill sets to the table early, in significant ways.

5. Adapting and responding. No two projects are alike. Adapt the system to each individual project. This (or any other type of system) will always be in a constant state of flux.

6. Optimize processes. Do not completely rely on any one way of completing a project. Rather, bring the most appropriate tools and procedures to bear on each project. Understand the underlying concepts and ensure that you use the optimum processes to solve problems.

7. Manage risks. Liability management is critical. Understand that by resolving issues early and proactively managing the process, you minimize your risks. Openly discuss and equitably allocate risks throughout the team.

8. Share information. Intellectual property is important, but it is not the priority. Be willing to share information to get the project done. Know and understand that free-flowing information is a basic requirement of an interoperable process. Without shared information, BIM and integrated practice are severely limited.

As your approach becomes more integrated, search for new ways to communicate the benefits that come from the process. Project teams and clients are beginning to understand the "big picture" issues that surround integrated processes. With a holistic understanding and proper information at the proper time, it is much easier for them to make correct decisions—no matter how difficult or complex.

Note: It would be presumptuous to assume that this list is all-inclusive or that 4SiteSystems is the only way to do this.

There are as many options as there are people in the built environment. This is one only way to integrated practice.

Let's take a look at some of the questions that you need to have answered as you become an integrated practice:

- How do we set our fees? How do we justify new fee allocations? What changes?

- How do I sell this? To clients? To staff? To consultants?

- How is a BIM-based process different, in a day-to-day office environment? Who is affected?

- What staff resources do I need to do this?

- Why would a client want me to do this?

- What savings come by implementing this process? For me? For my clients?

- Do I have to throw everything else out and start over? Can we still use AutoCAD (or Microstation or....)?

- How can we most effectively do this?

- My CAD people tell me that we can already do this with our current technology. Why are owners saying something else?

- Does anyone else even care?

- What's this got to do with architecture?

- We can do 3D drawings, and they look good, so...what's the big deal?

We will help you to find answers to these questions as we explore how 4SiteSystems works for us.

Leverage value

4SiteSystems is a mechanism for focusing attention on helping clients find certainty about their projects. It minimizes the wasted effort and inefficiencies that cost owners extra money. The process gets projects designed and built, on time and on budget, while meeting owner requirements. It gives owners unprecedented control of the life of their facilities.

4SiteSystems helps owners make decisions with more dependable information at the earliest possible time in the planning and design process. The goal is a process that makes decisions happen at the optimal time in every project. The process moves to the best solution for each specific instance.

By necessity, we describe the process in a linear fashion. It is not necessary for the process to be linear. Elements of the process can (and should) occur in different sequences depending on the project. However, the process often flows in chronological order as listed.

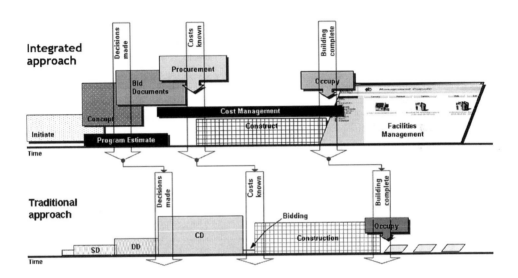

Timeline comparison—Using bim, you create more information earlier. Early information allows earlier decisions and greater control.

The Validation Process typically occurs for every project. You tailor the prototyping required, procurement approach, and construction methods to each engagement. The selected delivery approach determines when we move from a "model only" approach to composing bidding documentation. Bidding documentation can be extracted from any model—even the Concept Prototype.

Your objective in the Validation Process is to focus your efforts and thought on the important things. You achieve the most when you realize that 80% of project results flow from 20% of causes. If you focus on the issues that fall into the

> The Construction Prototype is not always required and the Procurement Phase can (and does) occur as an overlay to any of the other phases.

critical 20%, you maximize results.

People call this the 80/20 principle. By applying the 80/20 principle, you focus your energies on developing a high degree of confidence in your early decisions. You may not know how the final product will look, since design comes later, but you will create a dependable vision that, applied correctly, will closely match the finished product.

Many people put average effort into too many things. If you can focus your efforts on the critical items, you can dramatically improve your results. The Power of Sixteen Concept theorizes that efforts in the top 20% of an activity are sixteen times more important than the efforts in the other 80%. By focusing on the most critical 20%, you leverage your effort.

In project terms, this means that, if you focus on improving up-front decisions, you can put yourself in the position of maintaining the advantage during production—rather than spending your time focusing on construction documentation. You can achieve gains that are even more significant in your productivity if you take this one-step further and apply the 400% Rule.

The 400% Rule shows that if you replicate your efforts 5X in the top 20%, you will see your output increase by 400%.

Focus on the critical 20% with laser-like intensity. Exploit the successes that come from this focused approach. Then repeat the process. Over time, you will begin to see quantum gains in your results.

Validation

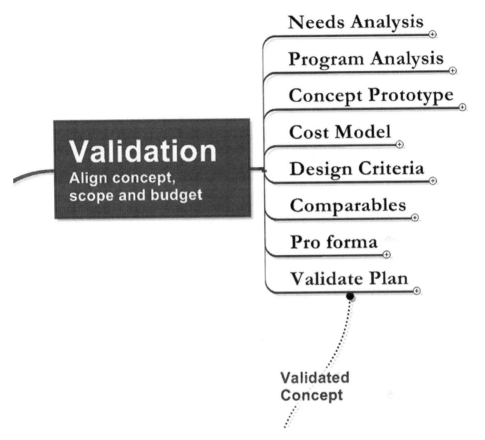

Frame the best possible solution to respond to the project. It is critical to envision the project properly. With the correct strategy and vision for the project, the phases that follow become easier to manage and more successful.

Align concept, scope, and budget

The Validation Process identifies the strategies for successfully designing, constructing and managing your facility, project, or process. The goal is to get a good, objective definition of quality; to define success at the beginning; to set appropriate expectations; and to develop solid project controls.

The size and technical expertise of your firm will likely drive your approach to Validation.

There are designers who cannot handle the technology or resent overlaying this level of control on their design process. This is counterproductive to integrated practice. By allowing these attitudes you may be positioning yourself for a sub-optimized process.

It is best if the designer, as a minimum, creates the concept prototype. Analysis and costing are also ideally designer functions, supported by technical experts and integrated databases.

The process works best when the designer uses the technology tools to consider alternatives, at the BEGINNING. Tapping into all of your firm's resources to get the Validation right will make sure that your projects start right.

Sustainability

The BIM process is by its very nature sustainable. When you work in a BIM process, you are by definition eliminating waste and reducing the inefficiencies that plague the building industry. As an inherently sustainable process, you are making a major impact.

BIM models give you many advantages over the traditional process. Your bim tools allow you to analyze energy use. The same is true for resource reduction, daylighting, and solar energy. You can make adjustments and try multiple options quickly and inexpensively. Using the same tools, you can also evaluate environmental safety, security, and a wide range of other issues.

Everyone should participate in this process.

We describe the Validation Process in a linear fashion. That is how books work. In practice, the steps move about. Design

Criteria might come at the same time or before the Digital Prototype. The Cost Model might happen based on the Digital Repository Model created in Needs Analysis. You change the flow to work best for you and your project. The parts should all be there. At times, they occur in different orders.

Needs Analysis

You start with a Needs Analysis that focuses on understanding the client's physical and underlying issues.

- Time—Document time goals, project performance requirements, flexibility, and restraints using scheduling and mind-mapping software.

- Constraints—Document financial, site, regulatory, and expandability issues.

- Mission—Document owner business requirements and any change management issues.

- Goals & Objectives—Document organizational goals, form and image goals, and functional requirements.

- Economic—Document management issues and financial restraints.

During this step, documentation can take several forms, depending on the level of project integration.

The status of the owner's BIM resources also becomes a factor. If your client has implemented integrated systems, much of this material may already be available within as-built grade bim models, IFC files, and other formats.

An owner who has implemented a BIM-based capital asset management program may have tightly integrated business process and facility asset information. If so, much of this effort revolves around data extraction and verification to support your project.

In the vast majority of situations today, owners have not created or implemented BIM nor integrated their archives and business processes. In this case, your efforts become much like any traditional fact-finding and site survey task, with the added requirement of processing the results to integrate with a BIM solution.

Documentation should feed to a data structure in a standardized format. The goal is to develop normalized data that easily integrates with rules-based planning systems.

By example: normalized data can take the form of a spreadsheet with predefined rows and columns properly named.

In many cases, access to such rules-based systems will not be available. In this case, you should manage data within a standard database structure, using a database-driven system such as a mind mapping solution or within a Type 1 Prototype.

Type 1 prototype—also called a Digital Repository Model (DRM).

A DRM is a bim structure that acts as a data container to hold project information and owner legacy data. The DRM acts as a bucket to hold available information and can take several forms. The advantage of using a DRM to hold data is that you can develop it further with minimal data loss or rework.

Program Analysis

In the Program Analysis, you break down client requirements and structure the data to get a clear picture of relationships.

- Physical—Diagram and understand project use, space requirements, relationships, and adjacencies.

- Schedule—Analyze phasing, occupancy requirements, and delivery issues.

- Function—Develop logic diagrams, block diagrams, and functional characteristics.

- Strategy—Develop initial delivery and procurement strategy.

Many options exist for this step. The main purpose of this step is for you to understand the project and to develop initial concepts for possible solutions. In the next phase, you will begin to create prototypical models to generate the parametric data required for detailed analysis.

In this phase, you become fluent with project requirements, owner issues, concerns, and limits. Therefore, you should use tools that give you this level of clarity. You should also school yourself to use tools that generate and manage data similar to those used for Needs Analysis.

We have found that the best tool for both analyzing and presenting this data is Mindjet's MindManager. This tool allows you to assess relationships and to communicate them through the entire team.

The downside is MindManager's lack of direct linkages to the bim prototype model.

Other possibilities for consideration are Trelligence Affinity, Beck Technologies DProfile and the Onuma Planning System (OPS). At the time of this writing, all three products are commercially available. These products feed directly to bim modelers.

Digital Prototype

The information from the Digital Prototype stage becomes the baseline for all future development. It becomes the "Objective Measure of Success" for the project. The goal is to define a solution that you can implement successfully within the owner's goals. This solution becomes the platform for studying and testing assumptions.

Type 2 Prototype—also called a Concept Vision Model (CVM).

A CVM builds upon the data and structure input to the Digital Repository Model (DRM) and your Program Analysis to create a virtual building model. In concept, this model is a high-level concept sketch. In a manual design situation, you would traditionally develop the concept using overlays and light tracing paper.

The CVM is a valuable data asset. Anchor it in reality. It allows you to add more and more information over time. Because of this, the data that goes into the CVM should be as accurate as possible. At the beginning, the information will be incomplete.

You can look at the process of entering data as a sifting process. As you start out, your data will be very grainy and coarse. Over time, you will sift your data to make it finer and finer. At some future point, you will have a virtual representation of the real world.

Understanding this process of sifting your information to make it more and more precise is critical to efficient and economical BIM.

Depending on the capabilities of your bim modeling solution, CVMs may range from a study of geometry with rules-based parameters attached—to virtual building shell structures created from intelligent planning objects—to a completely built-up virtual model with floors, walls, ceiling, roofs, et al. As a bim solution, you can extract great quantities of design analysis data from any of these approaches to the CVM.

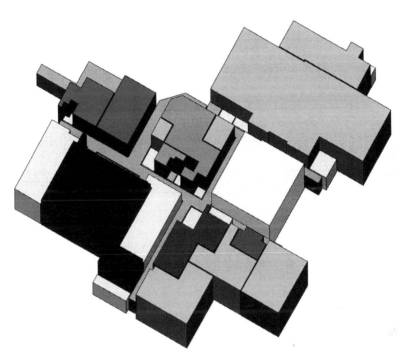

Crisfield, MD—Prototype for a school renovation. In this case, the CVM is a series of data containers holding educational specifications data.

Snow Hill, MD—Concept Vision Model for a church renovation. In this case, we based the CVM on an as-built model.

Site Data—the site information that you include in your CVM can take many forms. Your options range from detailed site survey to working with satellite mapping.

Google Earth data is georeferenced. It clearly includes context. It allows you to maintain your model within a consistent and repeatable context that others can work with as well.

However, it is not always high resolution. Aerial photography or other satellite mapping may show finer detail. It is sometimes not as accurate as a site survey (and sometimes you must be that accurate).

Google Earth usually meets the standard for granularity at this stage. You will likely find that Google Earth provides the best and most consistent level of site data to support the CVM-level model.

Model management—Underpinning the entire BIM process are consistent archives of owner information. Any system for organizing data must allow consistent and safe ways to store and find your information. Your data must be shareable, in a consistent and repeatable way.

In a paper-based system, management of information created libraries. In the BIM world, model servers are the equivalent. However, today model servers are nearly nonexistent.

As an individual firm, you will have to look everywhere to find one. If you find affordable model servers, you may find that they are either too restrictive or cost too much for day-to-day productivity.

Develop a strategy for model storage and sharing that will let you move to a model server solution, in the near future. Today, the best you can do is to add model servers to your ongoing learning list.

Keep up with what's available and look at them all.

Sketching and presentation—many designers believe that you cannot do conceptual design as well on the computer as by hand. They fear creative losses. They look at the computer as a production-only tool. They do not commit to the effort to learn how to design using digital tools. They cling to the belief that they will always be able to sketch by hand and have someone "draft" it for them on the computer. They could not be more wrong.

The trick is to find a tool that you like, and to learn how to use it well. You made an effort to learn how to sketch with pencils or markers. You have to make an effort and to learn how to use these tools, as well.

Today's best tools allow unprecedented levels of freedom while eliminating unnecessary work. Used correctly they allow you design freedom while overlaying design constraints. They offer the ability to break the rules, knowing what the rules really are, and knowing the impacts of your decisions. When you complete the design, you have eliminated a lot of the mundane and repetitive production work.

> We sketch in our bim modeling solution and Google's SketchUp! We use a variety of photo and illustration products from the beginning of every project.

Cost Model

The Cost Model is a financial planning tool to help the owner understand project cost constraints. We develop the values in a process similar to the "Design Phase Program Estimating" support used by agency construction managers and pioneered by George Heery, CM Associates, and others in the late 1960s.

The entire validation process happens quickly. For typical projects, the entire validation process takes about two weeks. Few projects take longer. The Cost Model comes together without slowing anything down.

The Cost Model relies on quantities extracted from the prototype model. Since we are usually working with a CVM at this stage, missing quantities are projected using rules-based tools and our internal knowledge base. We then use a combination of RSMeans' Cost Data, DC&D Technologies' D4Cost, and internal cost data to arrive at cost projections.

When used collaboratively with the owner, the Cost Model has proven to be a highly effective tool for controlling project

We rely on a hybrid process designed to create useful data without delaying the project.

Our team leader for this stage was the chief estimator for a medium sized general contractor, prior to working with us. He knows about deadlines and pressure from the contractor's viewpoint. He maintains our internal cost data and does a lot of the hard work to pull this together. This lets us turn the Cost Model around quickly. It allows us to review and adjust. He makes it possible to overcome a lack of integrated parametric estimating tools.

You will need to develop your own hybrid estimating system, at least for the short run.

Dependable parametric costing systems are not readily available at the time of this writing. Vendors have started to focus on this area and given time, systems that directly link to your bim model will be available. When integrated and interoperable parametric estimating systems become available, you should change. Until then, this is one area where you can make major improvements to your projects, even though they require a level of personal intervention.

You make it happen.

outcomes. The goal is to create a model, which includes cost placeholders for all anticipated costs in the project. This model becomes a design constraint. This model then becomes the objective measure of financial success for the project.

Factor scheduling and phasing into the Cost Model. Without understanding phasing, estimates can miss critical costs. Without a delivery strategy, it is easy to miss both opportunities and dangers. Without an understanding of when construction operations will occur, risk management is more complicated.

Start scheduling and strategy assumptions in the Needs Analysis step. They should both be included in the Cost Model. By this stage, you should have a concept for the planned procurement and implementation of the construction. You should also have a clearly drawn timeline.

> We usually do this with a scheduler such as MSProject. We then export schedule data to Mindjet's MindManager for additional procurement and implementation analysis.

Make cost management one of the most important pieces of your process.

Good online estimating tools are available at a reasonable cost. With judicious application of construction knowledge, common sense, and a willingness to ask questions and learn, you can improve your estimating process. Depending on your resources, this may require you to associate with a good estimator. It may require you to get additional cost management training. It may require you to hire someone with estimating skills. However you do it, jump into cost control.

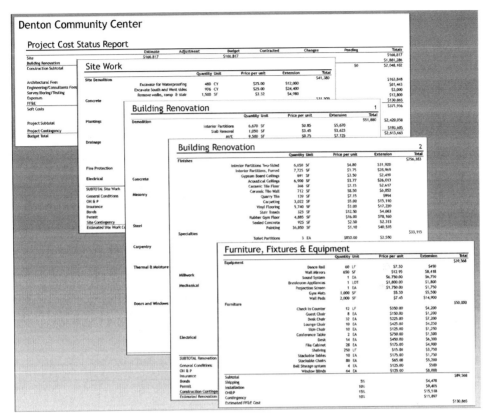

Base the Cost Model on data from the CVM and parametric rules-based cost data.

Design Criteria

Design Criteria is the process of documenting the project's strategic decisions and the assumptions that drive costing and the prototype. Here you focus on the tools that make the BIM process so powerful. This is where you run tests and analyze the model.

Assumptions

The prototypes, models, and analyses developed to this point are "parametric." Define these parameters by using rules of thumb, knowledge databases, standards, accepted practices, and experience.

You are able to pull a great deal of information from these parametric objects. As we discussed earlier, if you are designing a kindergarten classroom for twenty children you can—with a high degree of certainty—project the number of desks, light fixtures, and toilets. You can project the square footage required, as well as ceiling, walls, and floors. You can project most of the "things" that make up the classroom.

A mature bim solution allows you to embed these parameters. The embedded parameters can be data—lists of items tied to a measurement. Alternatively, they can be intelligent objects that have graphical representations. A chair can look like a chair or can be a description of a chair. In either case, your bim tools give you the capability to test and analyze the object.

These embedded parametric objects form the heart of the project. They establish the scope, scale, and quantities. You can estimate them. You can analyze them. However, they do not include everything that makes up the project. For that, YOU fill in the blanks.

The goal of the Design Criteria step is to document the assumptions that you make when you fill in the blanks in the project's parameters. You are creating "placeholders" that represent items that you know from experience will be required. Without these placeholder assumptions, things will be missing-you will create a flawed analysis.

Wicomico County, MD—Validation Phase image extracted from BIM data. Such images are often mistaken for output from 3D modeling software. Data from this model populated the cost model and became the basis for funding designs by local, state, and federal agencies.

Comparables

Owners want to understand how their projects compare with similar projects. When you do not provide comparisons, your cost model will naturally be compared to out-of-context "cost per square foot" evaluations. It is likely human nature to test this type of information.

These comparisons will at best compare apple to oranges. Some will include site work, some will not. None will include project soft costs or interior fit up. These comparisons will make you look bad. They will not improve comprehension. They will get the owner worried. They will create confusion, not certainty.

Comparable analysis eliminates this problem. By actively leading this step, you help your clients evaluate their project based on standards correctly applied.

We use DC&D Technologies' D4Cost system almost exclusively for this step.

The system allows you to identify a group of similar projects. It then allows you to adjust the projects to local conditions and the projected construction time. Since D4Cost is a database-driven system, the project data is consistent and repeatable. You adjust the level of detail to the owner's requirement.

Pro Forma

The Pro Forma presents the client with the data to explore options for alternate approaches, reductions, and additions.

We selected the Pro Forma terminology to represent the partially complete nature of the data prior to this review and approval. In this step, you review and analyze project information with the owner. From this review, you make adjustments before finalizing in the Validated Program step.

Options

One of the goals of the Validation Process is to frame the project with the components required for successful implementation. Successfully achieving this goal, results in a solution that closely matches the owner's requirements.

An all-inclusive solution such as this provides the optimal approach to visioning a project. However, real-world issues (budgets, political restraints, etc.) often require compromises and adjustments. Because of this, it is critical that cost reductions, potential additions, design options, and other alternate approaches be included in the Pro Forma.

Validated program

Your final product is a validated program that defines limits and possibilities, and guides the steps that follow. The Validated Program can take many forms, depending on the client and situation. Ideally, an interactive Web-based document presents the data without losing the connection to the integrated environment. For many clients, a formal series of documents including a bound report, a presentation for public use and a series of databases and bim models in the project Web portal are required.

The solutions in the validated program serve several functions:

- They become the space use program and measure of success for continuation of the project.

- They become the statement of owner requirements to guide the design architect.

- They become the basis of procurement documents for design/builders.

Build trust

The dictionary defines validation as—to establish the soundness of—to corroborate. By completing the Validation Process, you have confirmed owner requirements. You have used building information to give the owner a high level of certainty. The level of trust that this builds places you in the position to act as the owner's trusted advisor. It makes you a valuable resource.

Because of this, you have options. You have the option to continue through Design and Construction. You have the option to transition into a project or program management role. Alternatively, you have the option to move on to the next Validation, handing the project off to others for implementation.

Existing facilities

We have already built up much of our world. In most areas, you have to work with existing facilities. Existing structures and owner legacy systems are the norm. Is there an 'easy' way to start, in this environment? Is it possible to start a bim project with an existing building, economically?

Let's look at several scenarios:

Existing conditions

Some architects and owners have looked at their existing facilities and abandoned all hope of changing to BIM. The cost of creating existing conditions models has been their excuse for not implementing BIM. The reality is much different. With a bim solution, existing facility models are economical.

Here is what you will find when you dig into using bim for existing facility owners:

Multi-facility owner—take a phased-in approach to developing as-built models for these owners. It is possible to create prototypes for a large number of facilities located throughout the world, very rapidly. These prototypes can hold whatever legacy information exists (areas, coordinates, program data, and planning rules).

Prototypes established this way become ideal candidates for rules-based systems. They can be upgraded to include geometry and detailed facility data. Ideally, every project undertaken once you create the first prototypes will use a BIM approach. As you renovate or replace facilities, the prototypes will become more and more precise. Over time, the owner will have built a real BIM system.

Renovation projects—these projects come in all shapes and sizes. No matter how renovations are developed, they all include some level of field review, diagnostics, and existing conditions documentation.

If you do much of this work, you have learned to take archived as-builts with skepticism. They are usually inaccurate. They are often uncoordinated and are usually not up to date. Often they represent several unconnected renovation projects that require you to piece them together.

Because of this, you usually field check, verify measurements, and create base plans from scratch—even if the owner provides you with electronic as-built documents.

You can design your BIM process to stop this mess. The bim as-builts that you create for the renovation project becomes the ideal first prototype. It, for the last time, aggregates the flat as-builts, acts as a library for owner information and creates a starting point for further design.

Millions of square feet of this type of model have proven that they are economical within standard fee and time limitations.

Multi-building installations—projects within multiple building complexes can touch nearly any building or use type that you can imagine. They can be renovations or new. They can involve infrastructure, or not. They operate as a microcosm—a world of their own. In this environment, the capital improvement plan is king.

Budget restraints often force these owners to focus on one project at a time. Deferred maintenance is a never-ending problem. These owners face a dilemma of where to apply limited funds. They often use architects' services to design a specific renovation or new project, period. It is rare for these owners to undertake a comprehensive program that fixes everything at once. You will usually be faced with a specific need that might have any number of follow-up needs.

If the owner has implemented a BIM process, you can interface to "plug-in" discrete projects. If not, BIM offers a number of possibilities for positioning these clients to move their facilities to BIM.

Today most owners do not have an integrated system in place. They have not implemented BIM. Usually the owner is wrestling with issues of conversion costs and development of standards. The owner may understand the potential benefits, but legacy restraints keep him or her from getting there.

In most cases, you will find that the best solution is to develop a master model with simple placeholder prototypes. You can then place your project in the master model and develop it using a bim solution. Then, as the owner develops additional projects, the framework is in place to grow the master model.

You will have successfully completed your project using the technology and created a path for the owner to build a BIM solution over time. This allows your project to move through design and construction into operations and maintenance. You leave the owner with a BIM framework that is sustainable and economical. They may not know how to use it, but it is a first step. It creates an opportunity for you to work with them to begin the transition.

When owners learn they can directly use your models to connect to their capital budgeting and facility operations processes, the framework that you created becomes valuable. At that point, the architect that can plug into their new master model becomes more valuable. In fact, it may make you indispensable.

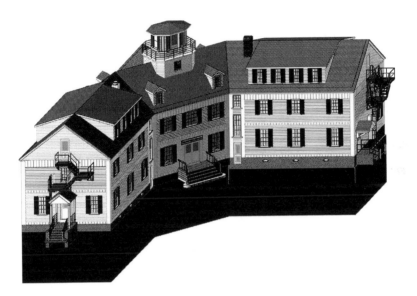

Atlantic City, NJ—With a mature bim solution, you create as-built models that far exceed the information and accuracy of any flat as-built—for about the same cost. As-built models become the ideal archive for digital information.

Design Prototype

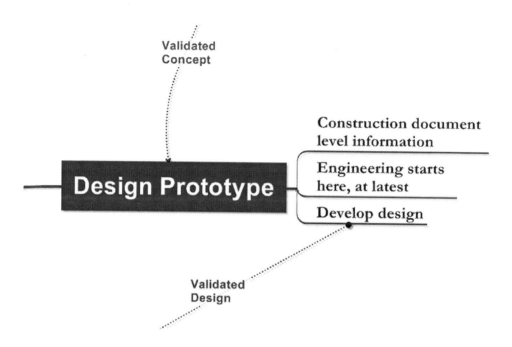

The Design Prototype Model is the second step. It is central to the process.

Type 3 model—also called a Design Prototype Model (DPM)

To most people the DPM is a "normal" bim model. You develop the DPM based on the decisions reached in Validation. The DPM most closely matches the models shown by vendors or used in a nonintegrated virtual building model environment. The models that you have seen have probably been DPMs.

The DPM may flesh out the Digital Repository Model or the Concept Vision Model. It can also be an entirely new design direction in response to the Validated Program. You and the owner decide how to proceed with this step. You have a number of decisions:

The first decision concerns the design solution.

- Is the concept in Validation the best solution? If so, you continue to add detail to your Concept Vision Model until the DPM is ready for the next step.

- If not, you use the constraints from Validation to create the best design solution.

- You have an additional option. Some projects are too large, too complex, or require special handling. For a variety of reasons, a large firm or a "signature" designer may be required. In this case, the Validation becomes the framework for managing the design. As the owner's trusted advisor, you transition to other roles.

The second decision concerns implementation. What is the best format for constructing the project?

- Do you have a constructor that can work from the model? If so, you are really integrated. You likely do most of what this book recommends daily. You built the DPM to allow for integration with the constructor. Your model includes the basics to support 4D and 5D. You model all systems with this in mind.

- Would some level of design/build be best? Earlier we discussed using the Concept Vision Model and Validation data for bidding design/build. With the DPM, you can take this a step further. With the DPM, you have an ideal tool for reducing design/builder uncertainty to achieve better bid results and smoother projects.

- Will the process look a lot like a traditional design/bid/ build? You will have to produce public bidding documents. You will likely comply with a rigid review process that has defined submission requirements. You will concentrate on building the model to a level that complies with your submission requirements.

You may find that your Concept Vision Model already includes all required Design Development documents—as soon as you compose your views on standard sheets. With a bit more effort you will have 50% Construction Documents.

You will create a well-thought-out plan for how to integrate consultants. You tailor your plan to the implementation approach. Much as in the "normal" process, you tailor specialist support to the project. You ask questions:

- What support is required to produce an excellent project?

- How will I integrate consultants? Have they integrated their internal processes?

- Can they work with my models? Can I integrate their work?

You should also consider the level of design analysis and data sharing that will happen in the project.

- Do your analysis tools require any "special" data?

- Must you fill in extra data fields in objects to use online tools?

- Do you need to place layers or zones in a certain way to ease future development?

BIM is about making early decisions. You should think ahead about your models. If you plan to analyze your building for sustainability, you should address this up front. The same is true for any analysis tool.

This is a place where "barreling ahead without a plan" can really work against you. Too often, those new to BIM have gotten far in the process, only to find out that much of their work was for naught. They could not use the model for the purpose intended.

The process relies on creating prototype models that contain the right information for each stage of the project while looking forward to future needs. You arrive at this step in an instant, from the perspective of the overall process. Yet the DPM is critical to success. It must be well conceived and built to a repeatable standard. It must support what comes next.

Gear the design prototype model toward creating biddable documents. Include the detail needed to support that goal.

Context

The built environment is complex. In an ideal world, you look at absolutely everything that affects your design. BIM gives you the tools to focus on an almost limitless range of issues that influence your design in this world. You are able to assess the affect fenestration options have on users. You can know the cost and energy implications for every solution you try. You are able to analyze the response to an attack or an accident—as you develop the design. All of these (and many more) are possible with BIM and integrated processes.

Scenario-based planning

Earlier in this book, we discussed the Onuma Planning System. We looked at how rules-based systems support BIM. OPS also supports scenario based planning on an enterprise level. By integrating verified data with clear visual images, the system allows fact-based simulations.

Knowledge from many sources integrates to simulate events. You set parameters and the system gives you a simulation of what happens.

An example is the ability to conduct security planning with blast analysis that visually displays the effects on facilities critical to an owner's mission. Since the simulations are database driven you can look at casualties, extent of physical damage and costs to recover.

The ability to integrate this level of simulation allows you and your clients to study the effects of decisions, well before programs are set, drawings are committed to paper or you pour concrete. You are able to "know" context in real time.

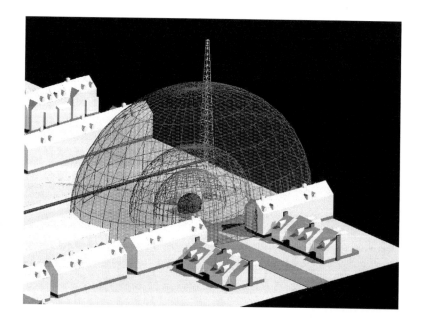

Major strides have been made in simulating Crime Prevention Through Environmental Design (CPTED) issues due to the pressures that developed post-9/11. By integrating CPTED principals, properties of destructive devices and facilities data, systems now exist to predict outcomes at a high level, before a terrorist strikes or tragedy occurs.

The goal is to create the safest environments possible, while supporting and enhancing an owner's primary mission. The environment heavily influences performance and behavior. By understanding and correctly manipulating the environment, you positively influence behavior and improve performance and security.

Safety and security depend on both physical and operational issues. A physical solution without proper operational changes will likely fail. Operational changes in a "target-rich environment" may have marginal results. Operations integrated with physical changes, assessed early in the planning process is what integration is all about.

Following the principles of crime prevention and emergency management helps you to create a balanced environment where security and emergency response complement design issues. By applying CPTED principles and techniques, appropriate behaviors are encouraged, inappropriate behaviors are discouraged, and emergency response capabilities are greatly improved.

You can use BIM as a tool to understand the environment and to visualize and quantify options and their effects. BIM as-built models provide security consultants with the information that they need to evaluate conditions and make recommendations. Models, when integrated with GiS, allow effective safety and security analysis from remote locations when conditions prevent on-site access.

The process begins with an understanding of your client's mission. The security consultant must understand what the client does and how they do it. This is a fundamental step in developing a comprehensive integrated strategy. The adage "one size fits all" does NOT apply to security and emergency response planning. What works well in one situation often fails in another. Each facility has its own unique context and needs its own equally unique plan.

There are codified standards in use for safety and security planning. They inform a rules-based system. Be careful when using rules-based systems in an automated design approach to safety and security. Used without knowledgeable professionals you run the risk of "garbage in—garbage out" in this area. Personal intervention assures that the output of the rule-based system correctly resolves contextual and operations differences.

You should help your clients' create their strategy based on their real needs, not on a generic security product. The security consultant recommends tactics to support the client's overall safety/security strategy. You should also help them to focus on tactics that are appropriate in their specific situation. These tactics should provide long-term performance and value.

Careful use of your BIM models, scenario based planning systems and security professionals allow you to support your clients' needs for a safe and secure environment. Tactics implemented without such analysis and understanding often fail from lack of support.

Knowledgeable security consultants integrate security and emergency response considerations into the design during the Initiate Phase. This assures the selection of appropriate tactics that fit with the overall security goals and actual facility use, early in the process. Used as part of the Validation Process, it has the effect of reducing redesign and additional fee costs.

BIM and security analysis are used to develop an emergency response plan that an owner can use to respond to an emergency and then to return to an operational condition as quickly as possible. An effective plan requires an assessment that will:

- Identify and prioritize the assets to be protected

- Define the level of threats the organization and facility may face

- Determine the vulnerability to the identified threats

- Evaluate the risks (the consequences of a threat) to the mission of the organization and facility.

You translate this plan into actionable plans and goals. You design implementable plans. You create workable goals that support day-to-day operation of the facility.

By identifying issues such as these, the security consultant provides a performance specification for lighting. The style, type (halogen, mercury vapor, or metal halide), and location of the lights must still be selected by the owner and the designers.

One of the benefits of BIM is you can model these options and visualize them before you finalize the design. You can extract the costs of installation, operation, and maintenance so that the decision will take into consideration life cycle costs.

Knowing this information is an extremely important security consideration. If you do not maintain security tactics, whether due to funding or inaction, you lessen their effectiveness and they may even become a liability for the owner.

The process is the same for any other part of the design: First, identify the possible threats, then determine how the environment contributes to making the facility vulnerable to the threat, and then determine ways to mitigate the threat.

For every situation, there is more than one solution. There are many ways to reach the desired goal. It is up to the security

An example is probably the best way to illustrate how this works.

You are designing a new hospital. Parking for nurses is a problem because they work shifts and are often alone after dark in the parking lot. This puts them at risk. The question is how to make them safe?

Parking can be inside or outside of the building. The parking lots can be on any side of the building, close to the building or far away... These are decisions best made by the owner and architect as part of the design process. The security consultant's job is to find the appropriate security solutions for wherever the parking lot needs to be located. The question becomes how to integrate the selected tactics without interfering with the aesthetics and functionality of the design.

First, consider the issue of lighting. Lighting should be greater than two foot-candles with no bright or dark spots across the entire parking area. The color of the light is also important. It affects the aesthetics of the area as well as security. If people visually monitor the parking lot, it is important that they be able to identify colors. This means white light. Other requirements become important if surveillance is by CCTV. The requirement can also change depending on the type of cameras and systems in use.

This is but one small example of the security issues that need to be integrated into the design. There are other considerations, such as paving material and color, which affect lighting and the surveillance capability. How these surfaces wear and change over time also becomes part of the consideration.

consultant, the designer and the owner to determine the best solution. The beauty of BIM is that it allows you to evaluate alternatives early in the design. By developing and integrating security early in the design process, you truly integrate it into the environment instead of security being "bolted-on" after the design is completed.

With the traditional process, the bolt-on approach has all too often been the way most designers do security. The bolt-on approach is arguably responsible for many recent security failures. Integrated practice and BIM let you do security a better way.

Focusing your efforts to integrate security and other similar issues at the beginning is a very different way to start a project.

Owners embrace the process once they understand the level of information that you are providing about their project. Using BIM to study everything that influences a project, at the beginning, is invaluable.

Normally architects have floated an architectural concept and then waited to work out the details in Design Development or Construction Documents Phase. This is the root of many owner problems with the traditional process.

Construction Prototype

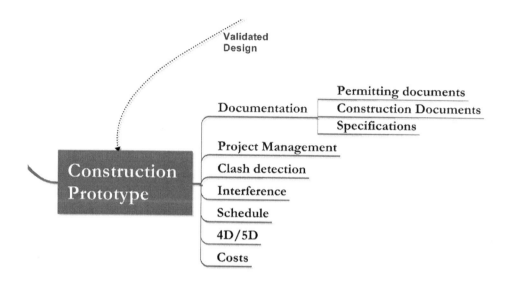

4SiteSystems is not limited to any specific construction delivery approach. You can use the process for all delivery methods. Tailor your services to the approach that is best for your client.

Type 4 model—also called the Construction Prototype Model (CPM)

Are you public bidding your project to general contractors?

The CPM continues the development of the Design Prototype Model. You have arrived at this stage with much of the production work already built into your model. Your goal is to maintain this advantage as you extract and compose bidding documents from your model. The level of detail and complexity that you build into the CPM allows automated extraction of construction detailing, schedules, and other documentation required for the bidding process.

This one process may require old-fashioned 2D drafting. However, this happens within the framework of the bim model, but in 2D linked windows.

Your bim tool should automate much of the process. The goal of this model is to produce clear, concise, and complete documents for public bidding, with a minimum of mundane and repetitive work.

Integrating other team members' data is critical to this prototype. As you move forward with the process, your consultant teams should consist of people who understand integration. They should be as invested in the technology as you are.

Today this is not always possible. In fact, today this is unlikely to be the case. Therefore, you may have to rely on translations via "flat" formats.

Plan your CPM production process accordingly. Some team members will be fluent in data sharing, some will not. You will find that you must take responsibility for the entire effort. Team members who work in a BIM environment are rare. So are architects. Fortunately, this is changing fast.

You should also consider the long-term use of your model.

Will the constructor use the model for conflict checking, or for 4D or 5D analysis? If so, it should be set up to allow this to happen.

Will the model become a long-term asset for the owner? Will you use the model for facility management and operations? At this stage, your model includes much data. Now is the ideal time to connect this data to a computer-assisted facility management system.

These considerations are critical to the process. If you are not thinking long range, you are not really doing BIM.

Procurement

Public Bid

Negotiated

Partnering

Procurement
Can begin after
Validation Process

As you have seen, the Procurement Phase can begin at many points in the process. You have tailored the process to your project. You have customized your model to match the best procurement method. You realize that the goal of the Procurement Phase is to define everything clearly. All decisions are integrated and available to bidders.

In the Procurement Process, you focus on clearly communicating and answering all questions, quickly and completely, no matter how obvious or mundane they seem. There are no stupid questions—especially during the procurement process. Every question that you avoid or miss will return as a problem—at the worst possible time.

You strive to eliminate all unknowns and uncertainties. You respond quickly and make dependable decisions. This has the effect of reducing "placeholders" and contingencies buried in bids. The result is bidding that is more responsive.

You freely share your data with bidders—ideally, by sharing your model. You even share the data through "flat formats," if that is what they require to do their jobs.

You understand that holding your cards close is the opposite of collaboration. You are here to get the best for the owner.

Clarity and simplicity are hallmarks of an integrated process. You arrive at the Procurement Process with a design that meets the owner's requirements. It has received a high level of cost and design control. You and the owner know that the design is on target. Whether you are negotiating with design/builders from a Concept Vision Model, bidding a design/builder from a Design Prototype Model, or bidding general contractors from a Construction Prototype Model, you are providing more data than is expected.

You couple that with a user-friendly project Web site to keep everyone informed. You fill in the blanks. You respond quickly and collaborate easily. This is how you get good bid results.

No matter how competitive the bid market is.

Construction

Agency Construction Management (ACM)

Construction Management at risk

Design/Bid/Build

Design/Build

Design/Assist

Construction

Interact with other professionals in the larger built environment. Focus on creating a highly integrated practice within a defined service area or branch out. Integrated practice, based on a clear understanding of BIM gives you the option.

The Construction Phase focuses on managing the project's outcomes within a collaborative process where all team members focus on creating sustainable and high quality results. In this phase, Cost Models developed in earlier phases becomes a tool for monitoring actual costs.

Type 5 Model—also called a Construction Model (CM)

You overlay 4D data (adding time) and 5D data (adding cost and management) to support the constructor. These models serve many roles. They act as archives for project data. They allow conflict resolution before fabrication. They act to measure performance. They allow you to manage the process while improving ordering and fabrication. With Type 5 Models you find problems and resolve them before parts are ordered, you move dirt, or you pour concrete.

Used in a fully integrated construction process, the Type 5 model will transition from conflict checking, through 4D and 5D into cost management and then act as the focus of all project documentation. At construction completion, this

Type 5 Model becomes VERY valuable for operations and maintenance.

Type 5 Models have special requirements. They interface with a variety of external databases to produce "real-world" results. You MUST build these models accurately. In fact, these models link to productivity and performance. Done incorrectly they can cause people to lose money and time. Done correctly they can save a lot of both. Know what you are doing before proceeding in this environment. You have the tools and ability to do this right. However, this is not the place for approximately correct.

They must reflect the full range of systems. When used for conflict checking they include structure and mechanical and electrical systems. When used for time analysis they include schedule data in all objects. When used for cost management, schedule and cost data become critical for all objects. Type 5 models may rely on some level of assumption. But, only as a last resort. The goal is to model actual conditions and costs. These models must closely simulate actual conditions.

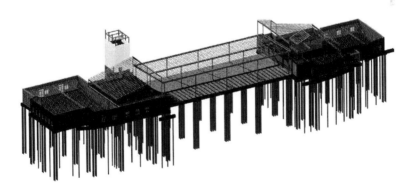

Salisbury, MD—Structural systems prototype created during validation. Integrated practice allows contractors to look at projects in more detail, faster.

Virtual design and construction

The construction industry is moving toward integrated practice. Contractors and builders are in the process of moving to BIM technology. They have realized the potential benefits. Owners are pushing them too. Vendors of bim tools have recognized that the constructor market offers them opportunities as well. Vendors have customized bim tools to support the building trades. This gives you options and opportunities:

1. Traditional—you can continue to act in a standard construction phase administration role. In this role, you optimize your process to support owners during construction. Your value to the constructor revolves around rapid decision-making, process controls, and collaboration.

2. Design/build—you can support design/build from either the owner's side or the design/builder's side. From the owner's side, you prepare procurement documents and transition to a program management role during the construction process.

   From the design/builder's side you fill the design/builder's architect role, producing permitting and construction documentation. Your value revolves around dependable results at the bid table, rapid response, and the ability to coordinate the team.

3. Support—the options above are not much different from the normal architectural role. You have the option to support the constructor with preparing Type 5 models and then managing the data through the construction process. A few innovators have worked in this role. Many of the constructors who are now integrating are working to build this capability within their organization. This is an obvious

need. It remains to be determined how companies will ultimately structure this role.

4. Integrate—Constructors are starting to integrate. You are integrating your practice. You have the opportunity to branch out and provide a completely integrated service or to find constructors who will work with you in an integrated mode. They are out there. Moreover, there will be many more in years to come.

Construction Phase integration is the subject for a book unto itself. Much literature is available from the established contractor-driven organizations. Search them out and read them.

You will find the possibilities to be a revelation.

Operations & Maintenance

Manage building space	Maintenance
Track occupancy and physical assets	Operations
Lease, rent, tenant and repurposing	Property Management

Operations & Maintenance

The processes to this point produces highly detailed and complete digital models that can be used for long-term operations, running simulations, and planning for the project's life.

Type 6 Model—also called the Facility Management Model (FMM)

The FMM becomes the archive for all facility information. You add data in the normal course of business allowing the model to grow over time. By including Web-based Facilities Management and long-term management of information, you are able to support owners though the entire facility life cycle.

Traditionally, planning, design, construction, and facility management are separate tasks in the life cycle of a building. From the perspective of the owner, separating these tasks resulted in additional costs and inefficiencies. Elimination of waste and inefficiency such as this is one of the most beneficial parts of BIM.

With BIM, you extract most building information from the bim model. With this information, you can automatically handle a much larger portfolio. Facility management support becomes a natural outgrowth of design and construction phase models.

FMM tools are available, but not in widespread use. You can use models at any level to populate these systems. You can use any model from the CVM to the Construction Model to populate facilities management tools. The FMM systems spin off management support data and become property management tools. These tools allow you to synchronize a bim model with the facility management database via the desktop or a Web server.

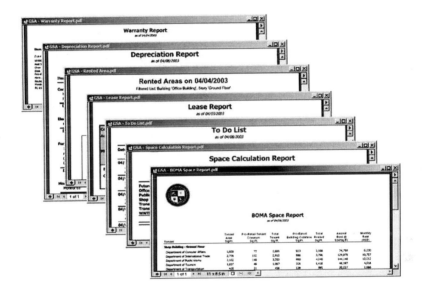

The data contained in your models allows the owner to analyze and monitor their facilities using tools such as Business Intelligence's Crystal Reports.

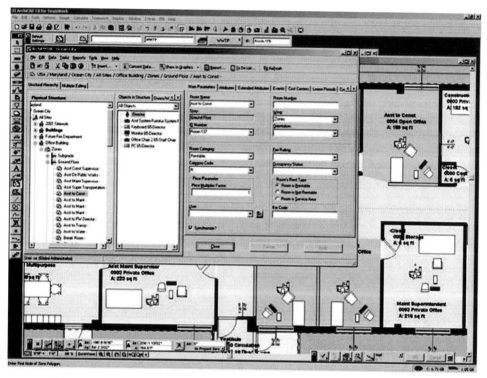

Integrating facility management forces you to take a long view, in order to maximize the benefits to owners.

CHAPTER 7

Firm

YOU STAND AT THE EDGE OF
a new world, where size really does not
matter. Technology makes it possible
for the smallest organization to compete
in markets once the sole domain of
large firms. The same tools make it
possible for large firms to deliver in
more markets. Both situations require
changes to how firms approach projects.
Both situations require changes in
structure, process, and attitude.

**Planning is critical to success in this
environment**

The world gets flatter by the day.
The line between the large corporate
architecture firm and the small firm is
becoming very faint.

This is happening because
technology has developed to a level that
allows the small firm to compete one-
to-one with the big firm. The small firm
can produce the same design quality,
the same images and the same (or
better) results. Using strategic alliances
and the tools available on the desktop
and on the Web, the small firm can
work big and compete with anyone.

The trick is to create a fully integrated organization that can use available tools to leverage your assets and skills. Create a well-thought out, well-planned and well-organized organization. Challenge preconceived notions and design the organization, much as you would design any other project. With such an organization, you can work smarter and create more with less.

The size of your firm is less important in an integrated practice. Small firms have real advantages in this environment:

- Simple implementation—A small firm can adapt quickly to today's way of doing work. They need to consult and convince fewer people to get things done.

- Easy to change—A small firm has a hierarchy that is easy to understand. Since you are small, you are already a flat organization and everyone does a bit of everything.

- Focused—A small firm can zero in on their individual skills and talents. They can focus on applying their resources where and when needed.

Large firms have their own set of advantages in this environment:

- Complexity—A large firm can bring a high level of resources to bear on projects that require a lot of figure-out time.

- Big/high visibility projects—A large firm can bring specialized skills from many directions to bear on large, multiphase projects.

- Big clients—Large clients often like to work with firms of similar size. A large firm can bring a level of comfort to such clients.

No matter how large or small your firm is, be flexible. Change easily. Tell the truth, no matter how difficult. Focus on your greatest skills and assets. Eliminate the mundane and boring.

Strive for excellence in everything you do—whether you are big or small. Think big.

Use BIM for projects of all sizes and types. Market the advantages. Clients will appreciate knowing more about their project earlier. Better cost control and predictability are valuable commodities.

Change the process

The traditional process for planning and designing facilities is under attack from many directions. Facility owners are tired of the waste and errors. The news media attack cost overruns and mismanagement of projects. Architects struggle with tight fees and standards of care that do not fairly assign risks and rewards. These attacks all spring from a process that has not adapted to the changes in our society.

Rather than using good business sense, architects have often fallen back on tradition and legacy systems to drive our decision-making. You can correct these problems; at least for your business.

The change can be revolutionary—discarding all that went before. You can start from scratch and invent an entirely new process. Alternatively, the change can be evolutionary—building on the good parts of the traditional process and replacing those that no longer work. You can integrate the old with the new. In either case, a different way of doing business is the result.

You have the luxury of deciding how you want to proceed. You do not have to have a grand and sweeping strategy. A business strategy should be more like a peek beneath the hood to look in detail at how you do business. This book does not focus on strategies that require you to start from scratch. It gives you strategies for what to look at and for folding current and evolving technology into the traditional approach to create new ways of doing business.

No architect likes limits on his or her design process. Limits seem like someone is imposing control. Limits seem like a bad thing. This becomes one of the major excuses for why architects resist process change.

Some say that this is where all future problems start. The fact is that architects have not done a good job of tailoring design resources to today's world. In most offices, the design process remains linear. This makes it difficult to integrate the early design process with document production and construction. It makes involvement in operations and management difficult at best.

Implementing BIM without changing the traditional architectural processes is fraught with problems.

Often designers conceive a solution and then hand it off to others to implement—a disconnect that is responsible for many future problems. The design process then becomes an open-ended research and exploration process—that uses too many of the available hours.

Since architects focus this research and exploration on design issues, they put off many decisions until later in the process. Design research and decision-making continue well into the documentation process. Moreover, since they do not make decisions at the optimum time, construction documents suffer and become the focus of profitability problems.

Critical decisions are being made too late in the process. By reworking your process to get good decisions earlier, you will have a major impact on your final product—and it will cost the least.

CHAPTER 8

People

 BY BETTER SUPPORTING YOUR clients, you become more valuable. You use your training and natural skills to synthesize information. You expand your ability to conceive and manage complex processes.

One of the major concerns of any organization is staffing. Staffing ideally revolves around supporting clients. Thinking back to the Toyota Production System, you drive the process from the client side—in this case the owner—not from production.

Since integrated practice is a rapidly evolving process, it requires different skill sets and different ways of looking at staff. It does not lend itself to the support hierarchy that most firms have created.

In an integrated practice, the staffing structure is flat—even senior staff participates at all levels. Integrated organizations are highly fluid. Pick the best team to get each project done.

You key all staff members, at all levels, into the process. As a rule, you move everyone toward more diverse skill sets. You are looking for the ability to synthesize data and problem solve within the framework that you establish. Obviously, different staff members will have specialty skills.

You balance loads to best use people's abilities. You will likely find yourself in a process of constant reorganization of the highly creative people who deliver the process. You will find it difficult to create organization charts in this environment—because they change so fast.

A chart done for a project today will likely be very different tomorrow. In integrated practice, people are much more important than structure.

Experience has shown that several types of people become important as you move forward.

Begin with a vision

Hire people that "get it"

People with vision are your first priority. If you are an established firm, these people will be your agents for change. If you are starting new, these people set the pace and define your practice.

For simplicity, we call this individual or group the "Change Agent." The Change Agent (CA) must be able to communicate the vision and overcome the complacency that comes from business as usual. The CA has or must build power sufficient to overcome any roadblocks to the process. Over time, the CA will ingrain the process into every aspect of the firm.

In a small firm, the Change Agent will wear all the hats. In others, a firm leader might be the CA with support from many others. Everyone is part of the process, from bottom to top. As you start out, a couple of your staff that "get it" might support the CA.

This team should work together to create a series of small wins. Leading by example is the single strongest approach to embedding integrated practice in your firm. As more staff members buy in, the process will reach a point where everyone is doing it, all the time.

At that point, the Change Agent must constantly reinforce the process. With constant attention, you can achieve the full benefit from integrated practice. In time, you will find that your staff will reach a comfort level with the process. You will find the best fit for their talents. You will create new positions as you become more adept at the process.

To deliver the 4Sitesystems process, we created a new job description—4SiteManager. A 4SiteManager is a project manager with the addition of integrated process requirements and a strong understanding of cost constraints.

The job adds the responsibility for actively finding places where you can eliminate repetition. It requires a hands-on ability to work with bim modeling tools and data structures to manage information. A 4SiteManager acts as the owner's advocate— looking out for the owner's interests, both short and long term. Flexibility, open-mindedness, and a broad understanding of the process are all hallmarks of a person who can be successful in this position.

A new process

One other staffing issue comes up when you talk about integrated practice. The issue revolves around today's "CAD Manager." In an integrated process, the position of CAD

Manager is redundant. Integrated practice to deliver BIM is not application driven. It does not revolve around enhancing or supporting applications.

If you focus this way, you will likely end up with less than optimum results. Worse yet, some firms that approach integrated practice and BIM with an application focus find themselves starting over after two years of testing and training.

CAD Managers need not fear for their livelihood, if they can change to a more integrated role. Technology-oriented staff members are critical to the process. Your CAD Manager may be your most technologically skilled employee. However, this process is not about technology. It is about integrated practice to create better projects and more satisfied owners.

Any system that you create or adopt must be simple. Successful systems rely on simple, easy to administer standards rather than the well-intentioned but highly complex standards that are the hallmark of CADD systems.

Maintaining your computers and software will be a continuing issue. The pace of change and innovation in this area will likely require more effort. Someone should systematically keep up with the latest innovations and products. This person should actively monitor blogs, participate in ongoing forums and test run new tools as they become available. All with the goal of making sure that you have the easiest and least costly tools for your projects.

Someone must create and manage databases. Someone must be able to create Web sites and, ideally, Web applications. A person with expert-level capabilities in your bim modeling solution is a valuable resource.

However, people fluent and fluid in many applications—not focused on only one, are the new standard. This may be your current CAD Manager—or not.

However you make this change, realize that you cannot abdicate leadership for integrated practice. Integrated practice using BIM is a core business process requiring executive-level leadership. It requires people who are powerful in your organization. Experience has shown that if you leave this to middle management or treat it as CAD management, you may experience mixed results. You may even fail in the process.

Leadership

The architectural profession is becoming more diverse. So are owners. Architects are finding that they cannot personally provide many of the services required today.

The popular conception that architects understand and can support all areas of the built environment is flawed. Nearly every project includes one or more specialists who would not have been included in the not too distant past. There are many "non-architect" professionals providing value in the built environment.

One of our goals when we created 4SiteSystems was to offer an approach that streamlined our ability to integrate nontraditional team members and the advantages of BIM technologies.

This occurs within a process that defines the issues, identifies costs and creates success strategies early in the process. You document decisions and design constraints at the beginning. You then work closely with constructors to get the project built on schedule and under budget. You then add long-term management of information to the mix.

With 4SiteSystems, you make integrating of specialist input easy.

As your process develops, you will begin to see the need to manage a wider range of experts. Psychologists, economists, security specialists, accountants, and others are required to support today's owner. Organizing a team that can deliver the full range of integrated services is difficult in most markets. Fortunately, architects' training gives them the ability to manage the process.

In order to deliver real value, identify individuals and firms that can give your team depth in the areas important to your clients. Establish alliances with them. Structure these alliances to allow information to flow freely. Take the lead to integrate them into the BIM process.

Even closely allied professionals such as mechanical, electrical and structural engineers will likely require support and education to help them to connect with your new integrated process.

Some of these professionals already work using processes that integrate planning, design, production and operations. Most do not.

As an example, industrial designers integrate more closely with the manufacturing process than architects integrate with the construction and operations of buildings. They understand and integrate production, shipping and sales.

If an industrial designer creates a product that cannot economically be manufactured, packaged, and sold, what happens? Is the same true for architects?

Integrated practice gives you a framework that focuses on adaptation and the life cycle of facilities. The process requires that you learn how to provide value within a context that is much larger than traditional practice defines. In an integrated practice, a firm's approach to staffing, clients, and consultants changes to coordinate with providing value in an information-centric world.

The changes require:

- A willingness to change business and design processes.
- A commitment to embrace new technologies.
- A high level of responsibility.

The process requires real leadership.

CHAPTER 9

Time

MAKING THE BUSINESS
decision to become an integrated
practice is a big step. It takes time and
commitment. The process requires
planning and forethought. Budget the
time to do it right.

At this point, let's take a look at a
couple of important questions:

- How can I successfully transition
  my staff to an integrated approach?

- How long should it take?

There is not one simple answer to
these questions. Every firm will be a
little different. Your firm has a different
mix of aptitudes, resources and skills
than other firms. Your firm works with
different clients, in different markets.
Because of these factors, the timeline for
making your change to an integrated
practice will vary. Fortunately, the steps
will be similar for most firms:

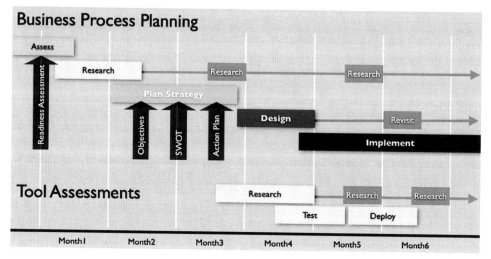

Manage the change. The process touches all parts of your practice.

Step 1: Assess readiness

Are you ready for integrated practice?

You start with introspection. Look at how you do business. Look at how you interact with your consultants and suppliers. Understand how your clients will react to a new way of doing business. Assess how you produce documents and how your staff may react to the change.

Some have found that the Strategic Forum for Construction's Integration Toolkit (http://www.strategicforum. org.uk) is a valuable guide for assessing their status.

The site includes an online assessment (http://maturity-assessment.dessol.com/about_you.php) that gives a measure of where you stand. If you use this tool, keep in mind that the measurement is in comparison to the construction industry in the United Kingdom. It requires interpolation for use in the United States.

You will find that the questions in the assessment offer a good overview of where integration is going. It will help you to understand areas where you should focus your time.

Other firms have gotten valuable data by having multiple staff members complete the maturity assessment independently. They have found value in measuring how well their staffs understand what integrated practice really means. It becomes a good starting point for further discussion.

You should budget several weeks for this process.

Step 2: Strategic Planning

You know that planning is important. Without planning, you react to problems. You never get ahead of the curve.

Start your strategic planning process by gathering information about what makes your firm special. Your goal is to understand your firm in the context in which you work.

- Clearly define your objectives for integrating your practice.
- Clearly document your financial conditions and history.
- Clearly document your client base and markets.

As part of this benchmarking and brainstorming process, you may choose to conduct a formal SWOT (Strengths, Weaknesses, Opportunities and Threats) process to identify and assess your situation.

> Do not begin a SWOT analysis without clearly defining and agreeing on your objectives.

When you do SWOT, you assess both the internal and external factors that affect your firm. Strengths and Weaknesses are internal to your firm and Opportunities and Threats are external to your firm. Keep them separate.

SWOT analysis enables a firm to focus on its strengths, to minimize its weaknesses, address threats, and take advantage of opportunities.

Take enough time to do your planning well. It will pay off in a big way as you move forward.

Budget a couple of months for strategic planning.

Step 3: Design your future firm

Begin to plan for the design of your integrated process. From the outcomes of your assessments, begin to look at the best ways to optimize your strengths and to mitigate your weaknesses. Develop a plan for exploiting your opportunities and defending against threats.

Break your plan down into bite-sized pieces and prioritize them. Write an implementation plan. Create a plan that builds step-by-step and allows you to achieve small, visible successes.

- What do you want to do in the future?

- How will you meet your strategic goals?

- What will your firm look like five years from now? Ten years?

Publish your plan. Talk about it to everyone you know. Make it important. You cannot put too much emphasis on your plan. It must become of major importance to everyone in your firm.

Designing your process may take several iterations. Use the structure outlined in this book and your own skills and experiences as a starting point.

> If you hold your plan close and do not involve your entire firm, your odds of failure increase dramatically.

Budget two weeks to one month for design.

Step 4: Implementation

Three or four months have passed during the planning and design process. Obviously, some will have completed the process much faster and others may take longer. Now you are ready to start, knowing where you are going.

Your plan is in place. You have a vision for your future. Now jump in and do something. Do not obsess about having a perfect plan. It is better (and more profitable) to spend your time doing something, even if it needs to change later.

This is not a static process. It will change over time.

> Use this book as your guide. Begin to develop your projects in a bim environment. Find new ways to create small successes. Tell your consultants about your new process. Market your new abilities and really work in an integrated way. Become an evangelist for integrated practice.

Find opportunities to share your successes, no matter how small. Keep talking and keep the focus on your plan. Get it done.

Step 5: Revisit

Integrated practice is not static. In fact, it can change every day. Because of this, your plan should be fluid and adaptable.

Integrated practice is a process change. As with any change of this magnitude, things will not be perfect. You will make mistakes and encounter barriers. The trick is to stay the course and adjust as you move forward.

You should plan a regular cycle for revisiting your strategies and solutions. Adjust them as you grow and become more expert in the process. As an integrated practice, become a life-long learning organization.

In the beginning, you will find yourself in a state of constant adjustment and correction. As you move forward, you should plan for quarterly or biannual reviews of your status.

Becoming an integrated practice takes time and commitment.

> You do not have to integrate everything at once. Do what you can, right now. Over time, you will be able to build more and more linkages into the larger world of BIM. Start with a plan and build your processes step-by-step until you are an integrated practice.

CHAPTER 10

Benefits

 THE CONVERGENCE OF BIM
and the growing sustainability ethic
offers architects an opportunity
to engage the whole spectrum of
building and project types in a richer
way. Architects can offer real value to
facility owners and their respective
communities.

This same convergence also offers
architects the best opportunity in
decades to reassert their value to client-
owners in what is their core market—
design.

Architects synthesize information
and manage complex processes at a
very high level. With these skills, they
are ideal candidates for leadership in
the building information modeling
process. Integrating their practices will
help them maintain their distinction
as a profession and avoid the creeping
irrelevance that comes from their steady
march away from risk.

Using process such as 4SiteSystems,
architects—both large and small—can
improve how they deliver their services.
These processes foster just-in-time-

decision-making, eliminating duplication and making the correct data available, when and where needed.

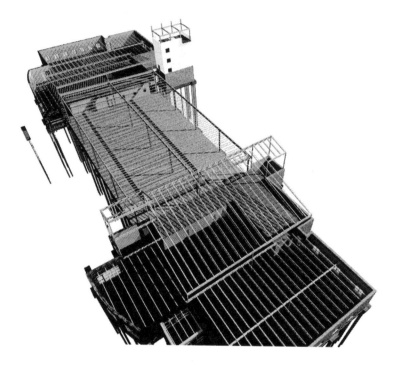

Salisbury, MD—Analyze your projects in ways that once took weeks and cost a lot of money.

Achieve more

When you deliver integrated services, you help your clients make better and earlier decisions, saving them money in the end. They will see direct advantages that do not come from the traditional design process. Your work begins to benefit all parts of the construction industry. Everyone profits.

Some of the benefits that come from integrated practice and BIM include:

Reduced risk

You engage owners earlier in a more collaborative way. You help them with early decision-making support and assurance of project outcomes.

- Virtual design and construction reduces risk.

- You are better able to withstand public scrutiny, the political climate and funding discussions.

- You detect errors—before they cost significant money, time or pain.

- You assure the necessary quality at the lowest reasonable cost.

- You deliver construction simulation before building—resulting in fewer misunderstandings, a faster bidding process, reduced bid-day surprises and less disputes and claims.

Managed change

- There are fewer change orders, fewer mistakes, and fewer losses.

- You simplify integration of new team members into the process (CPTED, Emergency Services, tools developers, psychologists, manufacturers, et al.)

- Diversify and compete in a wider spectrum of service areas and client types.

- Repurpose your work products for downstream reuse to support phased delivery.

Create clarity

- Study organizational structures, physical requirements, and operations issues in depth, early.

- Capture intelligence and rules. It helps you to begin the knowledge management process.

- Manage constraints to enable faster, better, and lower-cost outcomes for both yourself and your clients.

Improve profitability

- Projects have a higher percentage of senior staff time and much-reduced production staff time, resulting in higher effective multipliers.

- New projects experience 8-15% savings in project costs. Follow-on projects that reuse project data result in increased profitability of 8-35%.

- More accurate cost estimates at earlier stages.

Improve communications

- Create, manage and integrate high performance communications among owner, designer, constructor, and new and unique team members. Develop more effective and simpler collaboration tools.

- Build diverse teams in rapidly evolving and competitive markets.

- Foster full participation by all team members.

Efficient process

- You improve project control—you can better document decisions, consistently.

- You get more time and energy for design—fewer issues to "work out" during CDs. Better-coordinated documents and a revision process that is more efficient. Spend less time on drafting.

- You produce higher quality outcomes with fewer hours.

- You can build complex geometry. Work with up-to-date and real-time information. Create just-in-time imagery for your clients.

More sustainable

- The process is inherently sustainable.

- You build project databases designed to predict and manage future alterations. Data connects to the facility management database—giving a fast return-on-investment.

- Owners see direct advantages to their operations, which do not come from the normal process. They see why this approach saves money in the end. They can, at little or no additional cost, end up with easier-to-manage facilities.

- You integrate facility management and GiS for better long-term management and operations of facilities.

- You improve accountability.

- You improve efficiency and allow for a more diverse practice.

CHAPTER 11

Cautions

UNDERSTANDING THE PAST can keep you from making the same mistakes or doing the same work twice. With today's technology, you can create a more sustainable, interconnected environment, and profit in the process. Using tools and processes that eliminate repetition while maximizing the efficiency of your clients' facilities and operations, you become more valuable.

As you have read this book, you have explored the threads from the past that inform integrated practice. Alvin Toffler helped us to understand that "you cannot run society on data and computers alone." Buckminster Fuller's ideas still ring true. We really can "do more with less." Many of the concepts that have driven change in our world came from their vision.

Our understanding of their concepts has matured. However, successfully achieving their vision requires more than buying a new piece of software. Finding the right tools and adapting your way of doing business is critical to prosperity in this environment.

The way you design your practice will depend on how your business looks now and where you want it to go. You have looked at changing perceptions and explored how to design your practice to integrate with building information modeling and an information-rich process.

Every drafting room of the 1970s seemed to have a curmudgeon.

It was his (they were all male) job to keep everyone on task. His desk was usually at the back of the open studio (the studio had to be open, because that was the latest innovation).

From this lofty perch he could spot the malingerer and that worst of all offenders—the Pouche'r. This villain was responsible for lost profits, delayed drawings and the firm's general inability to deliver and make money.

Although always exaggerated, this characterization has been common. It is very likely that over-drawing and excessive detailing have been a problem since the days of the medieval master builder.

Step forward to today. The drafting room of 2007 is different. There are no drafting tables. The standard tools of the 1970s are museum pieces. Now, if you have a fast laptop or a flat screen monitor, a fast computer, a mouse and an iPhone, everyone should get out of your way.

You have the world at your fingertips. You can do it all.

Because of this power, we offer several cautions before you proceed with your exploration:

Sell the benefits

Architects face many dilemmas. They dream of designing the ultimate project. They strive for perfection. They work to stay ahead of the curve, because everyone else passes them if they do not grow.

They react by holding their cards close. They become afraid to take risks. Then they run risks by openly sharing their concepts and innovations.

Architects fear for their intellectual property, with good reason, since society puts everything that architects value on the line. When something goes wrong, their approach makes them an easy target. Architects have a lot to lose. Fortunately, integrated practice offers the solution.

It also offers confusion.

The complexity of the whole information modeling issue makes it easy for people to blow smoke—making it hard for good people to understand what is really happening. Bad information makes it hard for an owner to request what he or she wants and needs. It makes it even harder for an architect to figure out the best approach. This confusion results in people continuing to work the traditional way—even though it is not as successful as it should be.

You can step in and do the right thing. You can make the benefits happen for your firm. You do not have to tell the world about it, you just have to do it. If you sell the benefits, forget the technology and give your clients a great product, they will buy into it. They usually do not want to know why or how. That is why we created 4Sitesystems.

You will find that selling the technology is not a winning strategy. When you sell the benefits of what you can do that others cannot, your win rate goes up.

Recently I attended a presentation by a firm that is supposedly a "BIM Leader" with 300 employees. A principal and the firm's CIO gave the presentation. Between them, they made at least five glaring theoretical errors. Obviously, vendors had planted the messages to further their position. They use the software, but that is all.

Today I read letters to the editor resulting from a recent BIM article in a major architectural journal. Almost all were application centric. Universally they reinforced the notion "Since application x is not able to do it now it is not possible. So why are we raising everyone's expectations?"

Risk selling an integrated process without telling people how the technology works. When you prove to them that they can see their project earlier, can make better decisions earlier, and can be more certain about the outcomes, they will buy into the concept. They want the benefits; they do not care how you achieve them.

When you try to explain what BIM is, people's eyes glaze over, because it is not important to them yet. It is too complicated. Why waste energy explaining what it is? Just do it!

Owners have changed before

Owners of facilities have spent a lot of money to implement new technologies over the past thirty years. Typically, they threw away old systems and started over every time a new system or approach became the standard. Each time this happened, they had to bear the costs to resurvey, re-input and replace their entire system. The monetary costs were significant. They lost inertia, resources, and information. Alternatively, they ended up with halfway implementations and ongoing usability problems.

For owners, the information-driven approach represented by BIM and process integration may be the ultimate step in

The changes that occurred in the production and archiving of construction documentation is one example:

Owners historically archived ink on vellum and pencil on paper. When they needed data someone searched through the files and field verified their "paper" records—the time-tested approach;

They then moved to plastic lead on Mylar media. This change had minimal costs, since nothing much changed for the owners. In fact, this medium improved owners' archival abilities;

Then pin-bar compositing systems were developed, ushering in what would later become complex CADD layer conventions and creating major archival difficulties;

Then large owners invested in CAD (Computer Aided Drafting) on mainframes. Each station cost a lot of money and the technology that fostered this change was so new that few gave thought to the realities of archival data. Much data was lost due to format incompatibility and tape drives that quickly became obsolete;

Then the standard moved to CADD (Computer Aided Drafting and Design) on minicomputers. Archived data continued to be lost to software revisions and format incompatibility, floppy disks and Winchester drives;

More recently, the standard became personal-computer-based 2D CADD. Archived data continued to be lost due to lack of interoperability, complexity of standards and lack of long-term storage media. File systems became so complex and hardware dependent that it became difficult to access archives quickly;

Then a few owners moved to 3D CADD on laptops. Data is not database driven, not intelligent, usually not interoperable and does not comply with a single standard;

And now to BIM and integrated processes.

moving away from the "throw it away and start over" approach. It is a practical way for them to reuse their information over the life of their facilities. With interoperable processes, they can reuse their information rather than recreating it every time a new system comes along.

The goal is to find a long-term solution that moves away from the cycle of starting anew each time a new technology develops. With BIM, you maintain data in standardized and shareable formats that can be software neutral. Whatever new technology is developed can read and manipulate the data. That is why standards such as Industry Foundation Classes (IFC) are so important. Rather than starting over, you move to a cycle of reading a data file archived in an interoperable format.

Data interoperability does not solve the problem by itself. If tomorrow we woke up and every software product on the market could magically "talk to and understand" every other product, the problem would not go away. This is because in most people's experience, the problem revolves around archiving and recovery of information.

How often have you tried to open a file from version—X of your current software, only to find that you cannot open it with the latest version—Y? How many times have you found the floppy disk with the specification for a job you completed 5 years ago, to find that none of your machines have floppy drives? How many times have you tried to access a CD-ROM burned six years ago and found that it was unreadable? These are the day-to-day issues that often overshadow concerns of interoperability.

I hope that model servers with redundant backup will resolve some of these problems. In the meantime, your system should include strategies for keeping your archived data in usable condition. Otherwise, what good is it?

Owners demand change

The traditional project delivery process is fraught with lack of cooperation and poor information sharing.

Owners can no longer rely on the traditional checks and balances in the construction industry to assure outcomes, because the industry is too disruptive and undependable.

> Studies suggest that owners experience project schedule and cost overruns on 85% of all projects.

You can lay part of the problem on retiring baby boomers causing a brain drain. Everyone is losing seasoned staff at a rapid pace. Throughout the construction industry, knowledge resources are lost as experienced people retire. Every year it becomes more difficult to hire experienced, senior staff.

The loss of knowledgeable workers, inefficiency and lack of coordinated workflows plague the entire construction industry.

> Some surveys predict that 50% of all senior managers will retire in the next ten years.

As architects lose experienced people, the tendency has been to rely on task-based automation to correct the problems. The errors caused by the lack of senior staff and other problems worsen as architects do not find effective ways to capture knowledge and make it available to the next generation. Even today, other professionals are starting to do many of the tasks taken for granted as traditional parts of architectural services.

The loss of knowledgeable staff and competition from other professionals goes so far as to make some architects fear for the survival of the architectural profession.

In 2004, the National Institute of Science and Technology (NIST) issued a report titled *Cost Analysis of Inadequate Interoperability in the U.S. Capital Facilities Industry*. The report documented the fact that the current approach is not sustainable.

By correcting disjointed processes, NIST predicted savings of over $15.8 billion annually (1-2% of total industry revenue). Obviously, owners would receive the greatest part of these savings. NIST estimated that the owners' share of the savings is $10.6 billion. Constructors' share of the savings is an estimated $1.8 billion, with fabricators and suppliers saving an additional $2.2 billion. Architects and engineers' share of the savings is an estimated $1.2 billion.

Could future architects find themselves relegated to generating only project aesthetics only?

Rules-based systems and modeling tools enable other professionals to deliver high performance outcomes in many areas that many traditionally consider the realm of architects. One can argue that these services miss the subtleties and standard of care that architects provide. However, in some cases, owners are willing to live with these losses to avoid the problems they are experiencing in the traditional process.

Owner groups are actively working to correct these problems. One active owner group is The Construction Users Roundtable (CURT). CURT's goal is to "create strategic advantage for construction users."

CURT's documents have acted as a wake-up call to the architectural profession. They have offered a strategy for owner leadership in enabling change needed in the construction industry. One could argue that they are responsible for much of the recent focus on BIM and integrated practice in the profession.

In 2004, CURT issued a call to action white paper titled *Collaboration, Integrated Information and the Project Life Cycle in Building Design, Construction and Operation.*

In the white paper, CURT issued a firm and clear message—Stop the finger-pointing, litigation, and lack of accountability that seem to be business as usual.

In 2005, CURT followed up with a second white paper titled *Optimizing the Construction Process: An Implementation Strategy.*

In 2006, the American Institute of Architects (AIA), CURT, and the Associated General Contractors of America (AGC) began a joint effort to transform the construction industry. The leadership shown by owners, contractors and architects working in tandem is critical to the future of the industry.

This joint effort is one of the many initiatives looking at interoperability, collaboration, risk management, and integrated processes. Unfortunately, many of these initiatives are overlapping and disconnected from others.

Much as NIST identified losses due to lack of interoperability in the construction industry, there is much the same problem with implementation, as many organizations work to understand integration and BIM. The complexity and fragmentation of the U.S. construction industry makes interoperability, even at this level, a major challenge.

Even with these challenges and the new processes represented by integrated practice, BIM and rules-based systems, some architects seem only to be paying lip service to clients' broader concerns.

If architects do not do something, is someone going to come up with a way to integrate them out of existence?

By facing these questions head-on, you can find answers. You can design your practice to provide value and overcome the issues raised by CURT. Let others work on the big picture issues. For the rest of us, the problem has to be solved one architect at a time.

Simple, concise standards

Today, much of the energy associated with BIM goes toward developing standards for the future. Some ask—"Who really follows complex standards?"

Anecdotally, projects that attempt to follow standards are large, complex, high gross fee, high-gross-project-cost, government-funded ones. Yet, these projects make up a small part of the total U.S. construction market, even though they are often high-visibility projects.

There is a strong case for simple and concise standards. Without such standards, BIM might always be marginal technology and might never achieve its potential.

There are groups working to create a National Building Information Model Standard (NBIMS) that will act for BIM as the National CADD Standard (NCS) has acted for flat CADD. Depending on your clientele, you may never need to focus on NBIMS. NBIMS will be embedded in some bim solutions. Over time NBIMS will likely be one of the many things that just happen with any bim solution.

Standards are often not enforced. When a standard is not enforced, it becomes more of an impediment than it enables productive and focused work. This book is about doing BIM every day. It is about simple BIM. For BIM to be used successfully your standards must be simple.

If you want people to follow your standards, they must be simple.

Many of the highly developed standards intending to control the flat CAD production environment focus entirely on specific applications. Using them, in most cases, adds little to a BIM workflow. When you move to a bim solution, you can usually abandon them without penalizing your work product.

Offices wrote CAD standards with worthy goals in mind. However they tend toward complexity. They tend toward hundreds of layers, pen tables and proscriptive requirements. They make navigation and understanding difficult. You cannot impose systems that worked for one specific instance on all instances. They are inflexible. They are by their nature impediments to change.

A integrated process using BIM must be flexible and allow for easy transitions between projects, tasks and people. It needs everyone to understand, without a data table or rule book. It needs common and understandable names. When you start, define only a small handful of attributes. After completing several projects, look at them and throw away everything that was not essential. From what is left, you might have a BIM standard for your office.

Retain the advantages

Someday architects' processes will be highly integrated with construction. Someday you will routinely share models electronically with the entire team. Someday you may see bidding reduced to a profit auction with all other costs tied to the market. However, these are a future reality.

Today's reality is that even with an integrated process, you issue bidding and construction documents. In an integrated process, you have to get to the same places. The difference is that the work effort has changed.

A generic traditional process goes something like this:

- You start with Schematic Design creating design concepts for owner approval. This approval requires a lot of faith and trust, since you include very little real information beyond aesthetics.

- Next, during Design Development, you define and develop the project's systems. Up to this point, the process is in the designer's control. Outcomes depend on the designer's abilities and knowledge.

- Next, the process moves to Construction Documentation and a handoff to the production team occurs. You continue to make critical project decisions. The bulk of project detail is added at this time.

If the designer was able to get the required decisions and finished the design process under budget, the production team's work is simplified.

If not, they take the handoff with a big disadvantage. They find themselves having to reinterpret and implement the work of the designer. Sometimes with his or her close involvement. Sometimes without input, while trying to make up for lost ground against the design fee.

Is it any wonder that architects have cost overruns and errors in their documents?

With an integrated process, you reverse this situation. You arrive at the start of construction documents with much of the work done. You have made the critical design decisions and included them in the prototype. You have confirmed material selections in the prototype. Production templates are set to generate the documents—plans, elevations—sections—details—schedules—et al. All coordinated, labeled, and in your preferred formats.

If your engineers and specification writer use compatible systems, their work is coordinated, interference checked and tied to the project index. Your effort to produce construction documents comes down to cleanup and packaging. The production team does not have to reinterpret or wait for decisions. They assemble the documents. It is much more controllable and predictable.

Excess Perfection Syndrome

Building information models and shared information (interoperability) make it possible to replicate the real world in your computer. With enough time and energy, a model can have nearly as many attributes as the real thing.

Much of this information is already in the model and tools. This information costs little or nothing since it has been—"captured." You must then add information, since every model requires some level of customization to match an existing condition or to reflect the design.

You must have a plan for managing this information. At every phase specific information and detail is required to get the job done. In the ideal, you place this information in the model, nothing more, and nothing less. Over-building models with too much information results in lost productivity.

Over documenting can dramatically affect your bottom line in an integrated practice.

Check your ego

Today, architects are players in a very small part of the built environment. Much of the world works with almost zero interaction with architects, contrary to some architects' notions of their role in the process. Studies have shown that most people have never even met an architect. Studies have also shown that most architects tightly focus on the "traditional" core of the business and they pay little attention to what happens before schematic design or after construction. Strangely, many architects seem to think that the built world revolves around them. It does not, by a wide margin.

There is a much larger world of built things, where architects are never involved. Integrated practice opens up this world to architects. Owners have strongly asserted a need for better integration of processes. They see building information modeling technology as the means for streamlining the built environment from cradle to cradle. They are exploring how to correct the industry's problems.

Architects, to great extent, have abandoned the larger world issues to focus on design and construction. Because of this narrow focus, many do not see architects as critical to integration. BIM and integrated practice make it possible for architects to expand into areas where few of them have gone before. However, until it happens, a false sense of his or her place in the world can limit an architect's options.

Many do not realize how closely architects' skill sets match the needs of integrated processes. Integration is a team sport. Architects manage teams. Not only design teams. With these skills, architects are ideal candidates for leadership in the integration process. However, becoming leaders in this change will not happen easily. Owners, contractors, engineers and unlicensed professionals with technology skills are all exploring how to lead the process. These same professionals are questioning architects' ability to fill a leadership role in correcting these problems, since architects have generally not "stepped up to the plate."

At a basic level, Architects synthesize information and manage complex processes. Few can rival these skills. Applying these skills through integrated practice allows lets architects focus their skills to solve the problems that plague the industry. Step up to the plate and get it done!

Status quo

Cedar Island Marsh, near the Chesapeake Bay—BIM and GiS tools let you study critical environments to minimize your project's footprint and impact.

We designed this book to help you understand how building information modeling and integrated practice can change your life for the better.

The solution began to take form in the 1970s. The '70s were an era of confusion, conflict, and change. McGovern lost to Nixon in 1972, and by 1974, Nixon had resigned. Intergraph was getting off the ground and AutoCAD was not on the horizon. The anti-war movement was in full swing. The floppy disk and the microprocessor had recently appeared, but most of us were still punching cards—if we used computers at all. Most considered Toyota to be a cheap import aimed at those with limited resources. Ford Motors was the gold standard. Futurism was in full swing. The possibilities were endless.

I left graduate school at the height of a recession. Jobs were scarce. After nine months of looking, I got my first job in a "real" architectural office.

They were a progressive growing firm. They sharply focused on productivity and profitability and they taught how to carefully budget and manage projects. They were constantly looking for better and more profitable ways to do things. They accepted overlay drafting, paste-up, and any other hand methods that got projects out the door faster.

They were a very detail-oriented firm and were quietly controlled by one of the first Certified Construction Specifiers (CCS). He taught me to pay attention to the details.

The firm's senior designer would produce a sketch. The rest of us worked out the details. We eliminated the problems. As long as someone made the effort and spent the time to resolve conflicts, we picked up most of the problems in the process. As a fallback, the firm had people full time on construction administration to catch anything that others missed.

They did design/build and design/build/leaseback, but most of the projects were design/bid/build. My first project with an agency construction manager started in 1980.

In the mid-1980s, things began to change for the firm. The specifications writer retired, I left and they had to hire new and less-experienced people. People sued them—several times, usually for something that they missed. The construction administration department could no longer talk their way out of the errors and conflicts with the documents.

The senior designer started to accept only waterfront projects for close friends. He did not have the time to handle the details and no one with enough experience was available to do it for him. They went from a high-profitability, growing, and dynamic firm to a static one. They lost their momentum.

The principals were perceptive enough to know that they needed to change something. They hired a management consultant, who met with limited success. They tried mergers, without success. They made functional changes.

In the mid-1980s, I returned in a leadership role. My partners expected things to work just as they used to. However, it was not possible to roll back the clock. Now there were more and hungrier competitors. Economic conditions had changed. Staff expected higher salaries and clients were demanding more in less time. Computers were becoming an issue. The firm's inertia was gone.

Construction management and design/build had taught me that it is much more cost effective to have all of the issues examined as early in the process as possible. I knew that projects that were properly budgeted and designed within the budget had a much higher chance of success.

We hired a senior construction manager to work with the senior designer in an attempt to correct the problems. Rather than solving the problem, hiring the construction manager seemed to signal the end.

The partners resisted making additional changes and refused to fund solutions. As a group, they had tried too many things, without success. They took the—"we will try one, and if it works, we will talk about another," approach.

Computerization was becoming a problem. Partners' attitudes were—"You can try it if you want, but I will never touch a computer." A longtime drafter was "allowed" to try Cadvance, but only as long as it was profitable. The firm's engineers were trying AutoCAD and they hired a drafter who knew how to use Microstation on UNIX, so they tried that too.

After months of meetings, they authorized a group to find the best solution for a CAD system. We looked at everything on the market—worldwide. We concentrated on products that would work within an agency construction management approach.

We developed a rough business case for the process. In 1990, we found the technology that looked like it would solve the problem. We began look at how we could tweak our process to make it happen.

We ended up buying ArchiCad. It worked with our rough business case. We started with one seat. We trained two people in the week after we got the software. Within nine months, the entire architectural staff was using ArchiCad and we had five seats, with no additional outside training. A senior architect was using ArchiCad to prepare all documents. Drafters were using ArchiCad for construction documents. New interns were producing virtual reality fly-thrus after only two days on staff. The software worked.

However, things were not getting better for the firm. It became obvious that we could not correct the problems by buying new software. The projects done per the rough business case went well. The projects done in the regular way did not. Broader changes to the business operation were required.

The partners continued their no-technology bias and the firm splintered into disconnected studios. We could not reach a consensus about how to move forward. Organizational change was not possible due to too many legacy issues. By November 1996, the problems had reached an impasse and Design Atlantic Ltd was born.

As often happens, we resolved never to repeat the same mistakes. We resolved to use technology as a tool to create better architecture. We conceived a test platform for new ways of doing the business of architecture.

Do not let your firm go the way of the firm described above. Embrace change and do what is necessary to adapt to integrated practice.

Control your projects

"If you're not the lead dog, the view never changes," quipped Ian Thompson, vice-president of Standing Stone Consulting Inc. Ian's comment came on the heels of a meeting with a school superintendent to discuss how to structure the team on a new project.

The superintendent required a textbook approach and could not conceive of why a high school might need CPTED support. Safety and security were critical. However, the superintendent could not be convinced of the importance.

The meeting was one week before 9/11.

Sometimes you just cannot change a preconceived notion. Sometimes the local situation and pressures force people to make the wrong decisions. As a professional, you still have to try.

Over the years, how many projects have you seen that started with a flawed plan? How many were under-funded? How many were over-scoped? How many missed a critical piece that led to failure in the end?

A primary goal of integrated practice is to avoid this type of failure. These failures happen because of a small, easily correctable flaw at the beginning. Conceptually it is simple to correct them at the beginning. In practice, it is much harder.

It seems simple. You have to start right.

As we completed more and more projects, we saw a disconnected process. People were forgetting the basic equation. Moreover, problems usually resulted ....

We saw a typical scenario play out repeatedly—the owner hires an architect without really keying him or her into the fiscal realities.

The architect creates a design that responds to aesthetic requirements but misses the issue of sustainability.

They build a facility that is too large or too expensive for funding to support. The organization struggles financially to operate the facility and then (and only then) the realization occurs that they missed something...

As a profession, architects' process is rooted in tradition. As a group, architects give too much power to legacy systems when they should be making changes using good business sense. The days where an architect could design without connecting to the client's business systems have passed.

Technology is commercially available to allow architects to do a much better job at controlling projects, from the very start of every project. They no longer have to rely on manual linear processes to produce quality work. Architects now have databases, the Internet and BIM. It is time to become leaders in making the change.

PART IV

PROOF THAT INTEGRATION WORKS

Case studies

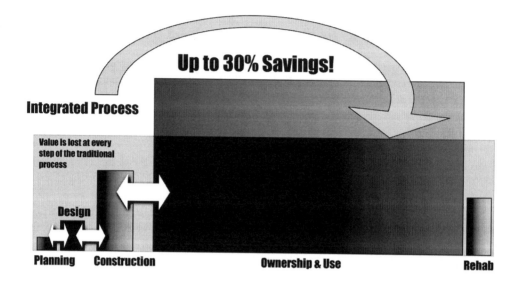

Either architects will lead the process or someone else will!

These case studies were all completed using 4SiteSystems. Over a ten-year period the process has shown to result in 8-15% savings on new projects and up to 35% in fee savings on repeat projects. Savings accrue to both the client and to the architect. These savings are the result of reusing information, having more (and better) decision-making information earlier, and better early phase analysis.

In general, the case study projects required fewer hours to produce high quality outcomes. They had fewer production problems since many of the issues were resolved well before they became problems.

CHAPTER 12

Fire Headquarters and Station 16

SALISBURY, MD

A volatile political environment.

A purchasing climate that favors design/build. A client concerned that things will drop through the cracks with design/build. A project stalled for twenty years.

Three architectural firms.

An opportunity?—Or should you run for the hills?

Several years ago, the Salisbury Volunteer Fire Company hired a fire station expert to help with the planning of a new headquarters and fire station. Working with a core group of firefighters, they created a design concept to meet the requirements of the company. The concepts included several innovations that were critical to the fire company's future operations. When the planning was complete, the project went into an extended site acquisition process that resulted in a land purchase in early 2005.

Cole+Russell Architects of Cincinnati, OH created the concept. Design Atlantic Ltd was the project's design/build consultants.

Summary

Salisbury Fire Department is a combined volunteer and paid fire company. This combination leads to a very passionate and committed organization. It can also lead to conflicts if the decision-making processes are not clear. With this type of Fire Company, simplicity and openness are vital. The integrated, information-modeling-based process is ideal in this situation. The project was an opportunity to advance an integrated process and information models to manage the procurement process.

Potential environmental problems required the exhibit design budget to be held until site issues were resolved. Design of this area started after construction was 25% complete. BIM and cost management allowed the delayed start without problem.

For Design Atlantic Ltd, the challenge was to manage the process without assuming the designer role.

The team of Cole+Russell of Cincinnati, Ohio; Davis, Bowen & Friedel of Salisbury, Maryland; and Design Atlantic Ltd worked well together. The process focused on using models to get the city high quality, decision-making facts. We used bim to validate decisions and concepts.

As time approached to complete the design and construction, influential supporters advocated for a design/build process, believing that this approach would give the city the best and lowest cost for the final product. The fire company was concerned that critical components might not happen. They also worried about quality control issues with design/build.

The fire company felt that a local architect should complete the project. However, they loved their expert's concept design. They believed that design/build was the best approach. They sought a way to manage quality while getting everything that they wanted in the project. They recruited a volunteer deputy chief to make sure it all came together.

The entire process took place in an open and accessible environment that allowed the client, the architects, the engineers and city staff to stay informed and involved. The process exposed and resolved conflicts and roadblocks. Since the process is fact based and simple, everyone was able to understand input and support the program as we moved forward.

Process Change

Concept prototype created from Cole+Russell's 2D concept sketches. The prototype allowed the team to evaluate the design to minimize conflicts that would affect pricing.

After much discussion, research, and attorneys' opinions, the city embarked on their first-ever design build procurement, and retained Design Atlantic Ltd as the design/build consultants to manage the process. The principal tasks were to:

- Make sure that the fire company got the station that they wanted. Keep the city's fire station expert involved. Validate that the concept met the city's requirements.

- Manage public bidding for design/builders. Define the fire company's needs well enough to control outcomes, while not stifling competition and design/builder creativity. A flexible process was the key.

- Manage project communications, conduct necessary public meetings, and make sure that everyone was well informed.

- Provide the fire company with detailed information to support properly budgeting and financing the project.

- Manage roadblocks as early as possible, so that the project proceeded smoothly. In this process, the fire station expert, Cole+Russell was the design architect. They developed the Needs Analysis and the Project Vision. It was critical to assign tasks to minimize overlaps and potential for conflict.

Owner comments

William Gordy, Deputy Fire Chief

Several years ago, the fire company hired a national fire station expert to integrate important training components into our new combined headquarters and fire station. When it came time to get it built, it was felt that we needed a local firm with expertise in the architect side of design/build to coordinate with our expert. We selected a local firm in that role, and signed them up as design/build consultants. I had worked with this firm on previous successful private projects.

Our political supporters believed in design/build. Yet, the fire company was concerned that critical components and quality issues might "fall through the cracks" with design/build. The architect's process has allowed us to manage both. Moreover, we got more than we ever expected.

The architect's process allowed us to control critical components yet retained the flexibility of design/build. The details provided by the building model gave us the resources to manage a complex financing package and to convince the city council to proceed with securing additional funding to meet the project's requirements. Being able to look at detailed information very quickly, early in the process has allowed us to manage our costs. Everyone clearly understood the project. In addition, we managed roadblocks so early that they never seemed to become a problem.

Features

- Collaboration and simplicity of Web-based communications.
- Early decision-making support and assurance of project outcomes.
- Design/build process managed to assure that the Fire Department got the quality that they expected at the lowest reasonable cost.

Challenges

- Public scrutiny, political climate, and funding.
- Multiple design professionals.
- Critical stakeholder requirements.

Benefits

The client had the option to procure the project in a traditional design/bid/construct process with the fire station expert firm acting either as the prime architect or as the associated architect to a local firm. The design team would have then completed the design process, prepared complete bidding documents, and bid the project to general contractors. On bid day, the client would have found out the project cost.

If the bids were within budget all would be well, the project would proceed. If the bids were within "reason," the project might have been "value engineered" to budget. However, if the bids dramatically exceeded the budget, the project would stall, a new funding cycle would begin and the client would have to pay the architect for redesign.

At that point, the architect's services would have been 75% complete and six months would have elapsed, a waste of much time and money. Moreover, is "value engineering" after bid date about value or about eliminating things?

Using building models and information management tools to validate the client's early decisions enabled them to predict costs more accurately, overcoming many of their risks from beginning a new project. The process used data and graphics extracted from the model to engage stakeholders and confirm project requirements, quickly and accurately. This happened in a much-compressed period.

The process reduced the city's up-front costs. The bulk of formal 2D documentation moved to the design/builder's architect and engineers. The early validation work positioned the design/builder with better and more dependable data. They were able to deliver more competitive and responsive proposals.

The process made the project flow smoothly for all concerned, giving the Fire Department a better project.

Metrics

Building Area	39,120 gsf
Site Development Costs	$1,747,138
Building Costs	$ 6,227,720
Total Construction Cost	$ 7,974,858
Costs/GSF	$ 159.20

Process

1. Confirm and document all decisions
- Monitoring and evaluation systems
- Deploy Basecamp project management site
- Publish MSProject schedule and export to MindManager.

- Goals, requirements, and standards review
- Design concept and strategy review

2. Concept design review to validate alignment of scope and project requirements

- Civil, structural, and MEP Engineering review of concepts and site
- Draft master Delivery Strategy
- Draft Program Estimate from 2D concept
- Analyze program with MindManager

3. Digital Prototype Model confirmed, analyzed, and visualized data. Site data from surveys and geotechnical evaluation

4. Cost Model from Design Prototype quantities and validated client goals

5. Design Criteria formalizing project strategy, approach, and assumptions

6. Comparables Analysis

7. Pro forma analysis, definition of options and cost reduction suggestions

8. Project validation review and recommendations

9. Procurement documents for public bidding to design/builders

10. Bidding, negotiation, and contract award process

11. Delivery process including final design, construction documents, and construction

12. Project acceptance and move-in process

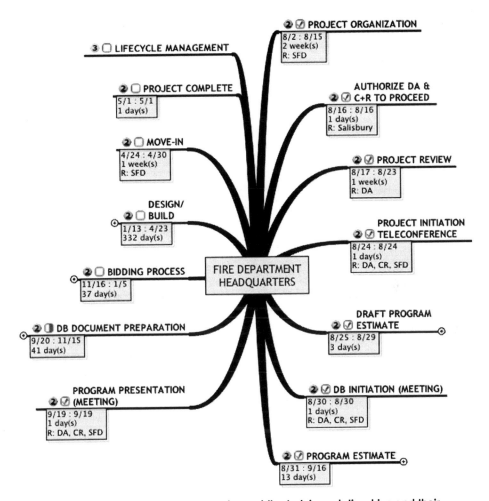

Mind maps support the process by rapidly studying relationships and their impact of phasing.

CHAPTER 13

Capital Improvement Program

Ocean City, MD

Small-design engagements sometimes take new and unforeseen directions. This project started like most—"design a new office and workshop." Over time, the project expanded to encompass georeferenced master models, Web-based facilities management, strategic planning, emergency services and a memorial.

An integrated process made it possible.

Municipal capital programs offer a diverse mix of projects. Traditionally design and construction of Ocean City projects happen piecemeal. The Town has traditionally ended up with projects that are not georeferenced. As-builts are inconsistent. In addition, they are often late and over budget. BIM processes have given the ability to respond to correct these issues without sacrificing efficiency, even in "one-off" situations.

Every project has different requirements. The Firefighter Memorial model allowed the Fire Company to coordinate contributions, donated services and public works department efforts.

Summary

The Ocean City Public Facilities Development Program uses high performance management systems and off-the-shelf technologies to support municipal requirements—efficiently and cost effectively. Integrated forward-thinking collaborative planning and design processes identify costs and success strategies early. All projects under the Program use an integrated, information-supported workflow. Overlaying everything is the management of cost constraints.

Integrated processes enhanced the ability to communicate issues and decisions to all team members, quickly and effectively. We organized the projects within a GiS construct, using readily available and mature design tools. Every project was georeferenced. Where practical and beneficial to the client, projects have been tested and prototyped using a wide range of analysis systems and interoperable tools. These studies allowed the Town to better envision, build, manage, and maintain their facilities.

The combination of the building information model interfaced with GiS and CAFM enabled the team to create a powerful environment to support the Town's ongoing capital development projects. The Town could visualize buildings accurately with three-dimensional modeling capabilities. The wealth of data included in the model allowed extraction of information from the very first concept. The building information model helped the team to identify costs and a success strategy very early in the design process and became a key part in the design practices and efforts to deliver the best quality customer services.

The Town of Ocean City, initially contracted to develop facilities to house the Public Works Department administrative and repair functions and to better control capital development costs. Estimated total construction costs in the ongoing program that began in 2000 are approximately $17 million. We have implemented the projects with a minimum of problems, under tight time constraints, and under budget. They have evolved to encompass public works and emergency services facilities throughout the ten-mile long coastal island community.

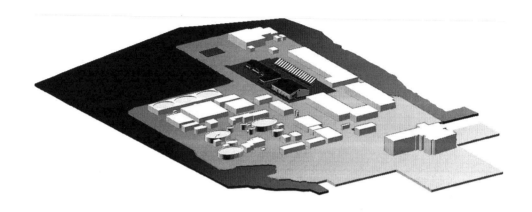

Central offices and maintenance shops models synchronized with CAFM. A master model allows direct connection of future additions to the system.

The Town of Ocean City contracted the team to redesign the fire company's headquarters facility and to develop a feasibility study for repair or replacement of an unmanned station. The team's ability to rapidly prototype concepts coupled with management of cost constraints, allowed the fire company to understand that program requirements would make their original concept impractical and very expensive. By clearly understanding the impact of the program on final costs, at this early stage, the fire company was able to redirect the project to avoid unnecessary redesign.

Contractor comments

Eric Milhollan, Project Manager, Construction Contractor

The design/build process worked great. It brought everyone (owner, architect, engineers, and contractor) together early. Everyone was given the opportunity to provide their expertise early, allowing for smooth changes and modifications that benefited the owner and the contractor. One example is the change from masonry on the office building to simulated brick. This gave the owner a credit, met the aesthetic intent, and eliminated a critical masonry requirement in a mason-poor market.

The documentation provided by the architect worked very well with Butler Manufacturing in coordinating the "non-standard" layout. The design/build process also enabled us to select the subcontractors we wanted and did not tie us to "down and dirty" low bids. The flexibility of the process, led to a profitable project—for us and for the owner.

Dean Dashiell, Construction Superintendent OCPW

We got a hell of a deal. The design was perfect. We were able to develop good relationships between the owner, architect and contractor early. This led to smooth communications and coordination throughout the project. This relationship has continued after "move-in" where the contractor has returned to fix or repair minor concerns. Key to this process is the owner having a representative who knows construction and how the parts go together.

The savings allowed us to clean up the utilities in the complex.

Owner comments

Hal Adkins, Director of Public Works

The projects have our fingerprints all over them. The process that the architect used for the design and construction of our offices and shops gave us the opportunity for detailed input to meet our needs now and gave us flexibility for expansion within the original footprint for future needs.

We got down to the details early. The early decisions resulted in significant time and money savings. The documents clearly reflected decisions. The architect's response to our input was a quick evaluation with clear graphics. Adding this to a fluid design process that eliminated the course of stop-go, stop-go too often found in the design community led to successful, intimate relationships between the owner, designer and contractor and allowed for relatively painless change solutions when necessary.

The benefits of the process are truly amazing. We conduct business in a quick and efficient manner. This approach allows us to comprehensively view and update data that would typically have been stored in numerous locations and media formats, an effort that consumes far too much time. Because building data is already contained in the models, the transfer of information from design and construction to facility management is streamlined. The process eliminates tedious, repetitive tasks.

Terry McGean, PE, City Engineer

Having the details to make early decisions paid off. The architect provided enough "worked-out" solutions to the needs of this complex renovation that our construction manager could come up with detailed estimates, quickly and accurately. The estimates opened our eyes and allowed us to reassess the needs and priorities of the entire emergency response needs of the community. We were on track to make some expensive mistakes.

Because of the flexibility and the team's access to world-class specialists, we were able to analyze the city's emergency response data and determine the best location for our emergency response facilities. The architect was then able to provide enough detail and data in the feasibility studies of the existing stations that we can now decide the best allocation of the money available.

Features

1. Facilities management and GiS integration to position facilities for better long-term management and operations
2. Successful design/build collaboration between owner/architect/contractor
3. Integration of new team members into process (CPTED, emergency services planner, Solibri, Butler Manufacturing, Marriott Corporation)

Challenges

1. Planning, design, and construction of facilities in a seller's market.

Time after time, newspapers have run stories of bids that exceed the budget. Often by more than twice the published estimate. The Town was no different. Costs were usually over budget and rarely were projects finishing on time. A different way to do business was required and the Public Works director was willing to try a new approach, even if it seemed risky.

2. Managing municipal facilities on a 10-mile-long barrier island.

Properly positioning and designing municipal facilities in a resort community is a challenge unto itself. Facilities serve the population surges experienced in every beach season, yet function economically year-round. The plan positions emergency services facilities to let firefighters and other emergency personnel reach all areas, quickly, even when the single access route is overloaded. Facilities have to withstand storms and a corrosive environment. In addition, budgets are tight and sometimes complex to administer. GiS, BIM, and other geospatial constructs offered the Town a way to manage these complex issues.

3. Managing a diverse group of clients and stakeholders in a small town with big assets.

City engineer—Public Works director—director of Emergency Services—volunteer fire chief, volunteer fire company—city manager—mayor—town council. These groups (and more) all have a stake in and strong opinions about how town facilities are designed, built and paid for. Needs and agendas vary and are sometimes in conflict. Communications and "knowing that we are right, going in" are critical to a smooth and orderly capital development program. An integrated approach with the right experts delivering an economical and efficient process was the solution.

Benefits

Integrated and BIM-based processes allowed the Town to benefit from the advantages of design-build, while retaining a high level of project control. The process began with virtual building models and detailed program estimates prior to beginning schematic design. We used the program estimates to manage the design and delivery process. The 10,121 gsf office and 16,720 gsf maintenance shop buildings were completed on time and well under the contracted budget. The only change orders were owner requested and resulted in several beneficial additions to the project.

Better project control and savings are possible with an integrated approach. The client and stakeholders have the information required to make correct, informed decisions, early in the process.

Collaboration

We integrated safety, security, funding availability, stakeholders' needs, and long-range planning into the process. A range of professionals including software companies, accountants, appraisers, Marriott Corporation, and Butler Manufacturing took part.

Unique to this team are integrated emergency services experts. The team created a Call Volume Study to help the Town determine optimal station locations and to best manage the growing call volume. The team also coordinated the Volunteer Fire Company's first strategic planning process and prepared concepts and program estimates for completing the Town's entire fire facility program.

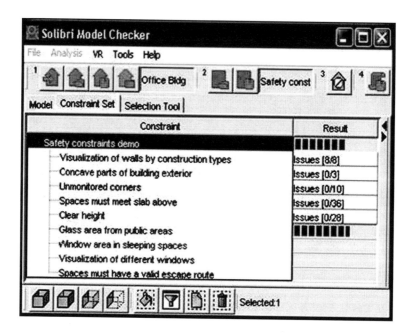

Use Solibri Model Checker to evaluate security issues. An automated analysis is one of the advantages.

Components

Public Works offices and workshops

Consolidation of Public Works administration and repair shop facilities were the focal point of a high-traffic public works complex. Project took place in highly seller-oriented market conditions where over-budget projects were the rule, rather than the exception. Savings to the owner—$260,700.

Metrics

Public Works Offices & Shop Building

Building Gross Square Feet	26,760 gsf (new)
Site Development Costs	$ 59,312
Building Costs	$ 1,822,888
Total Construction Cost	$1,882,200
Costs/GSF	$ 70.34

Emergency Response Stations

Buildings Gross Square Feet (new & renovated)	67,532 gsf
Site Development Costs	$1,361,000
Building Costs	$ 8,722,000
Total Construction Cost	$ 10,083,000
Costs/GSF	$ 129.15

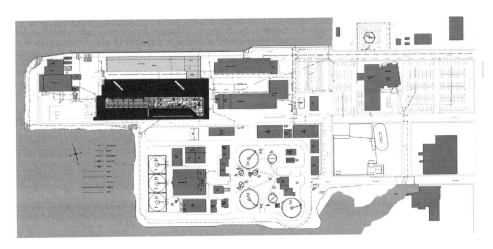

The complex centralizes the Town's infrastructure systems. A master model and master object library allow the system to grow over time while minimizing upfront costs.

Fire Headquarters Renovation

Rehabilitation on a constrained site. Required redesign to manage major shifts in emergency services delivery. Early decision-making process caused this project to be redirected to the new Midtown Central Station. Building will be rescaled to become a satellite Fire Station.

ArchiCAD7, Portfolio, AutoCAD, MSExcel, Solibri, Filemaker Pro.

Emergency Services Call Study

Review and analysis of current and projected emergency call patterns.

MSExcel, GiS data analyzed and presented with ArchiCAD8.

Emergency Services Site Study

Emergency response analysis and real estate assessment studies to identify available properties and to budget for acquisitions and divestitures within a highly built-up beach resort environment.

ArcInfo data, ArchiCAD8, assessment database, AutoCAD.

Volunteer Fire Company Strategic Master Plan

Extensive stakeholder input process, facilitated off-island retreat and worked with the Volunteer fire company to develop their first strategic master plan.

MSExcel, ArchiCAD8, MSPowerPoint, Adobe Acrobat.

Fire Station Feasibility Study

Overlaid data from other surveys, assessments, and call pattern studies with costing, program requirements, and facilities requirements to determine optimal program for providing emergency services facilities for the next twenty-five years.

ArchiCAD8, Portfolio, AutoCAD, Microstation, Adobe Acrobat.

North Island Fire Station

Design for larger equipment and staffing to provide timely service to high-rise beach hotels and condos in the northern end of the Town.

ArchiCAD8, Portfolio, Adobe Acrobat.

Off-Island Fire Station

Design to upgrade and expand an existing unattended fire station to accommodate live-ins and to react to current and projected personnel.

ArchiCAD8/9, Basecamp, MindManager, MSPowerPoint, MSExcel, Portfolio, Adobe Acrobat, AutoCAD, Google Earth, SketchUp.

Mid-Town Central Station

New headquarters station designed to remain in operation during natural disasters. This station also becomes the central support hub to manage high-volume support at remote locations due to extensive traffic blockages and other barriers during beach season.

ArchiCAD8/9, Basecamp, MindManager, MSPowerPoint, MSExcel, Portfolio, Adobe Acrobat, AutoCAD, ArcInfo, Google Earth.

Firefighters' Memorial

Memorial to fallen emergency service personnel located at central focal point of oceanfront boardwalk.

SketchUp, ArchiCAD9, PlotMaker, MSPowerPoint, Excel, Google Earth.

CHAPTER 14

Children's Theater of Delmarva

Delmar, MD

"We don't have much money. We do not have a site. We are still putting a board together. Nevertheless, we have a vision. We must plan for the next thirty years."

This is the challenge that the Children's Theater of Delmarva presented when they approached us in 1998. The Children's Theater allowed us to apply commercial off-the-shelf (COTS) technology and techniques that we developed to define a new organization.

This project is truly a labor of love. Founders of performance groups are often highly motivated and enthusiastic visionaries. Their energy and focus is critical to success. The founders of the Children's Theater of Delmarva created a unique and exciting program that is one of the community's tools for exposing youth to the performing arts. They offered the opportunity to design not only a new building, but also a new organization, using BIM.

We designed the Children's Theater of Delmarva (CTOD) to be an integral part of the community and to provide youth with education-oriented experiences that will enhance the area's overall cultural experience. The organization has successfully worked with a wide range of young people and adults to support this mission. They have operated without a permanent home and have survived in part by the generosity of those with existing facilities and by renting the necessary space.

The process documents, explores, analyzes, and models the end state. The goal is to define the steps that the group should take to reach their vision.

Summary

The first task was to develop a concept visualization model to generate public interest and attract funding for planning. With planning funds in hand, we opened the process to the community. Next, we created a concept vision model, extracted costing data and validated the theater's program.

The program validation required extensive research on comparable facilities and involved the directors of a number of successful theaters. Working closely with the theater, financial professionals, and the design team, we projected performance schedules, and income and expenses to create a plan for long-term funding. From this data, the theater was able to quickly raise development funds and begin negotiations for their preferred site.

A permanent home was crucial for long-term growth and continued success. The overwhelming success of the theater's signature educational show, "The Stand-Up," further supported the need. What initially began as six local children performing their special talent is now a mad dash to become one of the first fifteen to respond to open auditions for each show. A permanent home will allow The Stand-Up to grow from six to twenty-four performances each year allowing more children to perform in each show.

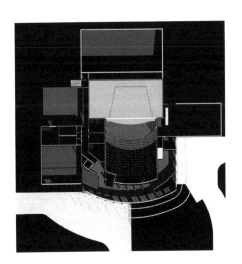 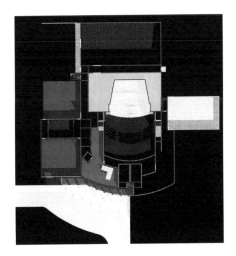

The facility's main theater will be a formal Broadway-quality theater with stepped, fixed seating. The black box theater will allow freeform performances within an open and creative neutral space. This will enable the facility to support two productions simultaneously; the main theater will host the larger production while the black box theater will host smaller house productions.

The facility will include dance studios, classrooms, administrative support, and all necessary "behind the scenes" support spaces. Studios for professional quality audio/video production and audio/video/lighting control are also incorporated. The theater will serve as an outlet for youth and encourage them to satisfy their passion while building skills in the performing arts, which in turn strengthens the relationship of the entire family through a tradition in the performing arts.

The CTOD could continue, as it is today, as a theater without a home for as long as the theater's founder is willing and able to produce shows, fundraise, and promote his vision. However, continuing in this manner is not sustainable. The community lacks a solid, Broadway-quality venue that can help youth grow and learn how to become better performers, in a caring, safe, and supportive atmosphere.

Due to the lack of a permanent home, the company has structured the CTOD's programs to make the best use of open-air venues and small community facilities. Participant growth and program needs have driven the CTOD toward creation of a permanent space to accommodate community demands. Without the proposed theater, the CTOD's ability to provide for after-school programs, theater camps, workshops, "at-risk" youth programs, and traveling shows is severely limited.

Owner comments

Carlos Mir, President and visionary

I had a vision, if you will, of a theater that would provide for children's productions and a venue for professional productions that would bring in money to support the children's theater program. My background is in events planning and fundraising—in getting people to provide things at little or no costs. However, I had no idea where to start.

I figured that seeing an expression of my idea would be a huge first step. I approached the architect and told him what I envisioned. I asked what we could create for minimal dollars.

What we got was huge. We got 3D renderings, a strategy, and a detailed estimate that gave a good idea of the direction we should go. They gave us legitimacy.

The community began to take the Children's Theater seriously. Producing successful shows without a home gave us the influence to move forward, and the graphics captured people's imaginations. The architect's next step was to continue in his efficient way to get us the most bang-for-the-buck. They produced an organizational development study that I was proud to take to patrons, banks and Rural Development to start the process of funding the theater.

You have to be thoroughly prepared when asking people and corporations to give large sums of money. I have great confidence when presenting "A Theater for Tomorrow," with its graphics, renderings, and detailed estimates and accounting. I am convinced this architect's process has allowed us to produce a far more complete report for less money and much earlier in the development process than normal.

W. Frank Brady, Board of Directors

We are a small group of people, parents largely, that is mainly concerned with providing a performing arts program for our children and the children of the community.

It is important to have a venue that our children's theater can call home. We have been quite successful as a theater without walls. This approach has been good for our children, but it is not sustainable. We really need a theater and a plan for generating the revenues to operate it, long term. Our understanding of the building process ends there.

The architect has been tremendous in providing us not only images and estimates, but also a long-range development plan that we can get our hands around. It is amazingly clear how the planned facility will meet our needs. We now understand what we must do to achieve our dream. Federal government funding sources have been very impressed with the work and the detailed plan. The study has already convinced a patron to commit the first $100,000 toward our project.

Features

1. Use of BIM at earliest phases of organization development
2. Use of BIM to chart the way forward in detail
3. Ability to study organizational structures, physical requirements, and operations issues in depth, early.

Challenges

1. Creating a plan for making a vision into reality
2. Funding for design, land acquisition, construction, operations, and endowments
3. Building support systems and awareness

Benefits

The ability to quickly extract and use the data from the model, coupled with an integrated process has allowed the CTOD early, complete, and detailed information to support financial projections and the development of the theatrical program. The board looks at costs based on accurate quantities extracted from the model. Even at this early stage in development, the group's producers and directors can analyze sightlines and visualize backstage traffic flows using the project's virtual building models.

Process

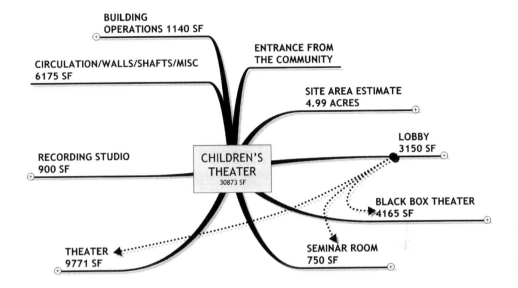

BUILDING
OPERATIONS 1140 SF

CIRCULATION/WALLS/SHAFTS/MISC
6175 SF

ENTRANCE FROM
THE COMMUNITY

SITE AREA ESTIMATE
4.99 ACRES

LOBBY
3150 SF

RECORDING STUDIO
900 SF

**CHILDREN'S
THEATER**
30873 SF

BLACK BOX THEATER
4165 SF

THEATER
9771 SF

SEMINAR ROOM
750 SF

Mind maps allow rapid exploration of space relationships. This tool is especially helpful for communicating and documenting group discussions and decision-making sessions.

Creating the framework for a new organization is a challenge. It is also a great opportunity. It truly offers a blank slate upon which to create. However, in order to realize the solution, the process has to involve a large group of local, regional, and national stakeholders. The team cannot approach the process as an ivory tower exercise. The process is collaborative. However, since little is in place at this stage, we had to create collaboration opportunities.

From the beginning, the core team included the founder of the theater, an accounting firm with a strong business planning background, the board of directors, parents, and our staff. We were able to involve directors of a number of established community theaters across the country to provide input and reviews. We received guidance from lenders, bankers, realtors, leaders of other non-profit organizations, and the youth that make up the Theater's lifeblood.

The Town of Delmar, DE/MD worked to pass a special exception for the project and to supply municipal utilities to the theater at the preferred site. The Palmer Foundation underwrote early development costs. They continue to provide guidance and funding. The Community Foundation of the Eastern Shore provides continuing input and holds the endowment for the CTOD. The Rural Development Administration has provided guidance and reviews. The owner expects them to hold the secondary note on the mortgage for the project.

The CTOD Board of Directors continues to raise funds and moving toward realizing their dreams for the theater.

CHAPTER 15

Armory Community Center

DENTON, MD

One good job leads to another. Design Atlantic Ltd had recently completed a nursing home renovation nearby when we were asked to interview for the conversion of the Denton Armory. The selection committee knew nothing about BIM. They knew that tight cost controls and certainty of outcomes were critical. Integrated practice and BIM became the deciding factor.

Rural Caroline County received an unused armory building with the agreement that they use the facility as a community center. The armory is an example of late-1940s military design with stepped parapets, cast stone trims, and projecting steel windows. The building was in poor condition due to deferred maintenance. The terms of the transaction required the county to maintain and restore the building, monitored by the Maryland Historic Trust.

The State of Maryland gave Caroline County the armory with many restrictions. The detail and accuracy of BIM models allowed management of these requirements without undue problems.

Summary

At its onset, the project required shell stabilization and accessibility upgrades. The county also needed facilities for recreation programs and a health club. However, minimal funds were available. The county staff was sure that they did not have enough money to do the project.

Caroline County publicly advertised for architects to assist with the design of their armory community center project. The County cited integration of BIM into the delivery process as the reason to select our team. They did not call it BIM, or think of it as integration, but they understood the benefits of early decision-making support designed to make their project successful.

Every project uses off-the-shelf (COTS) technology to leverage our abilities and the scope, even for the smallest renovation projects. These systems gave the county the tools to make early, informed decisions and to better plan.

A facility conditions assessment and a concept model were the first tasks. We then modeled repairs and a design solution. We used data from this model to prepare program estimates. Funding required the work to be limited to a portion of the project. We developed the portions of the project's model that included the funded items to a level that allowed extraction of construction documentation. We completed the project successfully from these documents.

Two years later, unexpectedly, we received a call. The project was again a priority. Needs had changed. The County administration had directed the Department of Parks & Recreation to move from the county central office building. They wanted to move to the armory. However, they wanted to make sure that the building continued to be a community center as well. The county's requirements had changed dramatically.

We were able to reactivate the as-built model, completely rework the entire project plan, and redesign the project in two weeks. The county received the decision support information that they required, quickly and inexpensively. All due to BIM.

We completely updated project programming. We updated budgets to match the new program. The county administration needed to know what it would cost to complete the project, so that they could allocate funds. In addition, it all had to happen fast.

We immediately deployed the project in Basecamp and began reassessing project requirements. Since Phase 1 was completed, our systems for project analysis and online communication had improved dramatically.

Parks & Recreation staff provided a list of their current and projected space requirements. Using MindManager, we were able to review and verify needs.

Interior view extracted from the design prototype. In Phase I, we extracted documentation to prepare construction documents. In Phase II, we reused these documents for validation and further developed for bidding and construction.

Owner comments

Sue Simmons, Director of Parks & Recreation

We selected this firm; because of the way, they focused on helping me to understand our project in the early stages. As a department head of a rural county, I do not often get involved in design projects. Each time, I have to ramp up my knowledge of design and construction.

The architect provided detailed information, from the beginning. The architect's approach helped me to understand everything that was going into the project. This has led to questions that I may not have asked in a "normal" process. In other projects, I got floor plans and sketches and had to assume that everything was included. When the details finally came, we often found that we needed changes. The changes then took a lot of effort, took too long and cost a lot. With this process, I was presented with the details and a clear picture of what was involved. If I wanted something changed, it was done quickly and I could see how it affected the entire project before I spent too much money. It allowed us to educate ourselves.

As a manger, I look for small manageable pieces that fit into place to organize and get things done. This small architectural firm works big. The principal architect is visionary and looks for the right tools to get things done in the most efficient way. The project manager has a strong construction background. The principal architect generates the ideas and creates the concepts and their PM gives me the assurance that the details are being worked out in practical terms. The relationship gives us a "yin/yang" approach. They turn with ease and adjust quickly. Larger firms are like dinosaurs or ocean liners; they take a long time and a lot of effort to turn or change.

Chuck Emerson, County Engineer

The community center project continues to progress very smoothly and efficiently. The team has worked great together. The communication throughout the entire process helps the work progress without many complications.

Being able to break out the elevator portion of the project to allow for early procurement saved a lot of time and enabled us to meet funding schedules. Being able to create a 3D model of the building was also a great asset in providing a clear vision of the project. Typically, the commissioners have to look at 2D plans and elevations and no matter how often you see those, it is hard to truly envision what you are going to get. The 3D renderings made it clear.

Contractor comments

Jay Yerkes, Project Manager

We had an excellent experience working with the architect on this project. J.J. DeLuca had recently opened a branch office on the Eastern Shore of Maryland and this was one of our first projects in the area. It was important for us to show that a big company out of Philadelphia could work well with the smaller communities of the Eastern Shore. The architect helped us do that.

From the start, the communication and information provided by the architect was clear and handled with quick turnaround. The architect responded to questions promptly and in an organized fashion. With a renovation, there are always hidden problems, but the architect had an excellent understanding of construction and the building, and worked with us to resolve any issue quickly.

An architect can play a part in the success of a contractor with a project and with their reputation. J.J. DeLuca made money on this project. The county awarded us other contracts without reservation. The architect and their method of business played a big part in that.

Features

1. Downstream reuse of building information models to support phased delivery
2. Cost and funding management
3. Process to front load project decision-making

Challenges

1. Managing evolving programmatic requirements
2. Coordinating phasing to match funding
3. Supporting owner decision-making and review process

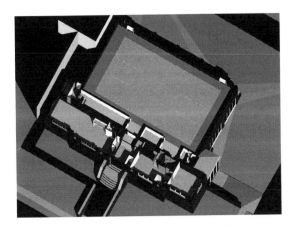

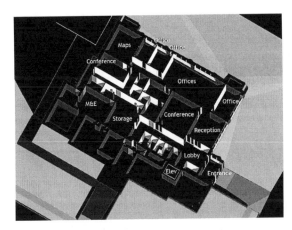

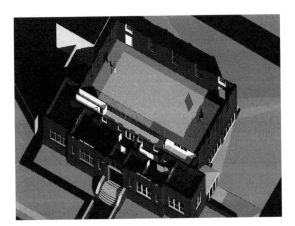

You can extract nearly any view from the model data. We used axonometric views to communicate the changed program at the start of Phase II.

Benefits

In Phase 2, the project was redesigned, prototyping the solution using the Phase 1 as-built model as a base. The process included:

- Digital Prototype model

- Cost model from model quantities and in-house and online Cost Databases

- Design criteria, assumptions, project strategy, and approach

- Comparison to standards

- Pro forma analysis and definition of options

The project's data was presented to the county to assist them in validating the solution. The same data was presented to the State of Maryland to lock in funding.

The restart took two weeks. The rework was finished faster than in the traditional process. Because of the as-built model from Phase 1, minimal fieldwork was required, saving the county about 50% in fees. Even with the lower fee level, this work was completed profitably.

Metrics

Phase 1

Building Area	5,120 gsf
Assignable Area	5,120 nsf
Site Development Costs	$ 7,680
Building Costs	$ 299,878
Total Construction Cost	$ 307,558
Building Costs/GSF	$ 58.56

Phase 2

Building Area	19,130 gsf
Assignable Area	16,430 nsf
Site Development Costs	$ 166,817
Building Costs	$ 1,881,286
Total Construction Cost	$ 2,048,102
Building Costs/GSF	$ 98.34
Building Efficiency Ratio	1.16

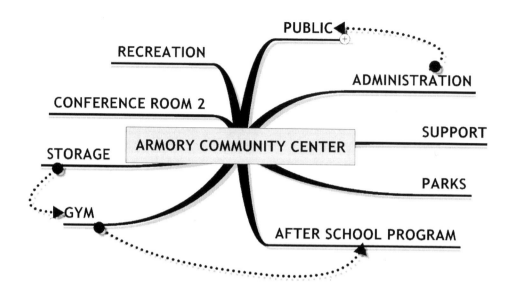

Mind maps consolidate early data collection processes. You use the data embedded in the mind maps for scheduling and cost analysis. They also allow you to write and organize formal text documents.

Process

The team started the process by field measurements and facility condition assessment. From these we created an as-built virtual information model.

At the same time, we began space programming with Parks & Recreation staff. From this information, we overlaid the as-built model with a concept design solution.

From the model, we then extracted both existing and proposed quantities to support creation of a program estimate. The program estimate is a parametric cost model tied to project assumptions, a delivery strategy, and a schedule.

The program estimate, coupled with the early detail from the model, became a tool for the county to allocate available funds. After reviewing model graphics and the program estimates, the decision was to construct the project in phases. Funding was available for Phase 1 only.

- Phase 1 was to include repairs to roofing and masonry, an elevator, accessible toilets and a few interior improvements. Due to scheduling constraints, the elevator was pre-purchased.

- Phase 2 required reevaluation of the owner's program and redesign to accommodate the changes. We designed the project to complete the remainder of renovations required for the Parks & Recreation Department in the basement, to create a recreation center on the first floor and to house support facilities on the second level.

We extracted graphics from the ArchiCad 9 model and composed them in PlotMaker 9 to produce construction document graphics for Phase 1. We publicly bid the project. The county awarded the contract, under budget. We created construction documents for Phase 2 fully in ArchiCad 10.

We completed construction of Phase 1 on time and with minimal problems. All submittals and changes are in our database project management system and in the model as as-builts. At the time of publication, Phase 2 is awaiting final authorization for bidding.

During the process, the county made adjustments and additions to expend available funds. The models made it much easier to manage the changes. The process reduced errors and construction problems—the county got an improved project. The Phase 1 models allowed the design team to reassess and redesign the project in a two-week period when Phase 2 started.

During construction of Phase 1, the Historic Trust requested a window analysis to support changes to the building's windows in Phase 2. We were able to supplement details extracted from models with up-to-date photography to complete the study, at minimal cost.

Because of financing constraints, the project went dormant for two years upon completion of Phase 1.

CHAPTER 16

Putting it together

 WITH AN INTEGRATED
process, you have the ability to create
new levels of service that extend
well beyond the traditional scope of
architecture. Architects have used the
technology, now called BIM, to complete
projects since the late 1980s. Literally
thousands of success stories at all levels
exist.

Now that you have read this far, you
likely have a good idea of the concepts
and scope of the change. You have a
vision for remaking your firm as an
integrated practice. You recognize areas
where integrated practice can give you
a competitive advantage. You may have
even started to build your own business
case for integrated practice.

You are proactive. You have a plan.

The cautious side of your mind
is also at work. You are concerned
with who will lead the change in your
organization. You are concerned that
your corporate culture will aggressively
resist the change—since you are
reshaping your organization and your

routine ways of doing projects. You do not know exactly where to start. An outsider might be able to guide you through the process.

Some organizations have found that bringing in an outside expert to coach them through the roadblocks and internal politics is the way to go. Sometimes a consultant can break the hold that vendors and application-centric technical staff have on an organization. Sometimes it takes someone who is not part of your firm to tell you the facts for you to believe them. Sometimes, you cannot see the big picture because you immersed in day-to-day problems. These issues led Design Atlantic Ltd. to offer BIM Coaching and Change Agent consulting services.

Assistance and support are available as you start the process. We tailor these services to your needs. We help you to clearly understand and relate to business challenges and opportunities. We help you to find solutions that value your unique skills and expertise. We coach you as you apply the right tools to identify and create sustainable processes that create value today and tomorrow.

A general overview of the support that we can offer includes:

Change assessment

The level of confusion and uncertainty that revolves around BIM and integrated practice makes some organizations question where they stand. Understand your level of readiness for integrated practice. We assist you as you assess your staff's awareness. We act as a sounding board as you identify and take advantage of challenges and opportunities. Integrated practice depends on the engagement of your staff and their willingness to adapt to change. We coach you as you lead the change.

Planning

Understanding and planning for the effects that this change will have on your business is critical to success. Define your business goals for integrated practice. With integrated practice in mind, understand your current capabilities. We support you in developing your strategic plan and business case for integrating BIM. We assist you with developing your project procedures to increase productivity and efficiency. Integrated practice focuses on using information to better support your clients. We act as a sounding board as you explore how your clients will receive value from the change. We coach you as you develop your personal approach to selling the process.

Strategy and implementation

Talking about integrated practice does not get work done. Your clients do not pay you for talking about process. Move forward to get the benefits from the process. We coach you as you execute your plan. We can help by filling in the gaps as you develop your resources, but that is not the goal. The goal is for you to build on your strengths to become the best and brightest in the business.

We act as a sounding board as you apply your new capabilities on projects. We help you with training and development of your team. We help you to identify and evaluate new tools and processes. Effective integrated practice becomes the way that you do business. We will help you to stay focused on the change.

Move your business beyond
information models

As author Robert Byrne put it, "Everything is in a state of flux, including the status quo." We live and work in an information-rich world, where the pace and volume of information challenges our ability to keep up. We need to do more and better with less.

This book shows the ways that we at Design Atlantic manage these challenges. Integrating BIM into your workflow involves many small changes that have big impacts. The goal of this book has been to cut through the hype to provide clarity about integrated practice.

You likely found that many of the concepts are familiar to you. This book describes what building information modeling is (and is not). It itemizes how BIM changes the way we approach design problems. It details the subtleties and small changes that you need in order to be successful. This book provides the information that you need to integrate BIM into your way of working.

Many people strongly believe that integrated practice and BIM can make you a better architect. By integrating technology, you can leverage your knowledge and experiences to concentrate your energies on your strengths—design and problem solving. This book details ways to make the changes without starting from scratch or "reinventing the wheel."

Resources are limited and you need to use them more effectively. Today's technology gives you the ability to make better decisions earlier, with more information. It allows you to better support your clients. Using an integrated practice approach and Building Information Modeling is the best path to becoming a 21st century architect.

I wish you "fair winds and following seas" as you begin your journey and make the change.

—Finith E. Jernigan, AIA

APPENDIX

Bibliography

Recommended reading for those who want more information on the subject:

Alexander, Christopher et al. A Patten Language. NY: Oxford University Press, 1977, ISBN 0-19-501919-9.

Caudill, William Wayne. Architecture by Team. NY: Van Nost Reinhold, 1971.

Cotts, David and Lee, Michael. The Facility Management Handbook. American Management Association, NY, 1992, ISBN 0-8144-0117-1.

Dettmer, H. William. Goldratt's Theory of Constraints: A Systems Approach to Continuous Improvement. NY: Asq Quality Press, 1997.

Duran, Rick. Understanding and Utilizing Building Information Modeling (BIM). NY: Lorman Education Services, 2006.

Elvin, George. Integrated Practice in Architecture: Mastering Design-Build, Fast-Track, and Building Information Modeling. Hoboken, NJ: Wiley, 2007.

Feldmann, Clarence G. The Practical Guide to Business Process Reengineering Using IDEF0. NY: Dorset House, 1998, ISBN 0-932633-37-4.

Forsberg, Kevin; Mooz, Hal, and Cotterman, Howard. Visualizing Project Management: Models and Frameworks for Mastering Complex Systems. Hoboken, NJ: John Wiley & Son, 2005.

Friedman, Thomas L. The World is Flat: A brief history of the twenty-first century. NY: Farrar, Straus and Giroux, 2005, ISBN 978-0-374-29279-9.

Fuller, R. Buckminster. Operating Manual for Spaceship Earth. Carbondale, IL: Southern Illinois University Press, 1969, ISBN 671-78902-3, Lib of Congress 69-15323.

Fuller, R. Buckminster. Intuition: Metaphysical Mosaic. Garden City, NY: Anchor Press/Doubleday, 1973, ISBN 0-385-01244-6, Lib of Congress 72-182837.

Fuller, R. Buckminster. Buckminster Fuller: Anthology for the New Millennium. NY: St. Martin's Press, 2001.

Fuller, R. Buckminster. Critical Path, NY: St. Martin's Griffin, 1982.

Gallaher, Michael P.; O'Connor, Alan C.; Dettbarn, John L. Jr.; and Gilday, Linda T. Cost Analysis of Inadequate Interoperability in the U.S. Capital Facilities Industry. U.S. Department of Commerce Technology Administration, National Institute of Standards and Technology, Advanced Technology Program Information Technology and Electronics Office, Gaithersburg, MD 20899, August 2004, NIST GCR 04-867, Under Contract SB1341-02-C-0066.

Gladwell, Malcolm. The Tipping Point: How Little Things Can Make a Difference. NY: Back Bay Books, 2000, ISBN 978-0-316-31696-5.

Goldratt, Eliyahu M. What is this thing called Theory of Constraints and how should it be implemented. Toronto, North River Press, 1990, ISBN 0-88427-166-8.

Hatch, Alden, Buckminster Fuller, At Home in the Universe. NY: Crown Publishers Inc, 1974, Lib of Congress 73-91509.

Heery, George T. Time, Cost and Architecture. NY: Mcgraw-Hill, 1975, ISBN 0-07-027815-6.

Hino, Satoshi, and Jeffrey K. (Fwd) Liker. Inside the Mind of Toyota: Management Principles for Enduring Growth. Portland: Productivity Press, 2005.

Koch, Richard. The 80/20 Principle: The Art of Achieving More with Less. NY: Bantam, 1998.

Kunz, John and Gilligan, Brian. 2007 Value from VDC / BIM Use survey, Center for Integrated Facility Engineering (CIFE) at Stanford University, 2007.

IfcWiki-open portal for information about Industry Foundation Classes (IFC), List of certified software, http://www.ifcwiki.org/ifcwiki/index.php/IFC_Certified_Software and Free tools that support IFC, http://www.ifcwiki.org/ifcwiki/index.php/Free_Software.

Jantsch, John. Duct Tape Marketing, Thomas Nelson Inc. Nashville, TN: 2006, ISBN 978-0-7852-2100-5.

Jossey-Bass. Business Leadership: a Jossey-Bass reader, Jossey-Bass, San Francisco, CA, 2003, ISBN 0-7879-6441-7.

Kieran, Stephen, and James Timberlake. Refabricating Architecture: How Manufacturing Methodologies are Poised to Transform Building Construction. New York: McGraw-Hill Professional, 2003.

Kotter. John P. Leading Change, Boston: Harvard Business School Press, 1996, ISBN 0-87584-747-1.

Kymmell, Willem. Building Information Modeling (BIM). New York: McGraw-Hill Professional, 2007.

Liker, Jeffrey K., and James M. Morgan. The Toyota Product Development System: Integrating People, Process and Technology. Portland: Productivity Press, 2006.

Liker, Jeffrey. The Toyota Way, McGraw-Hill, NY, 2004, ISBN 0-07-139231-9.

McKenzie, Ronald and Schoumacher, Bruce. Successful Business Plans for Architects, McGraw Hill, NY, 1992, ISBN 0-07-045654-2.

Nisbett, Richard E. and Ross, Lee. The Person and the Situation. Philadelphia: Temple University Press, 1991.

Rogers, Everett. Diffusion of Innovations. NY: New York Free Press, 1995.

Roundtable. The Construction Users, WP 1202 Collaboration, Integrated Information and the Project Life Cycle in Building Design, Construction and Operation, pub Aug 2004 and WP 1003 Construction Strategy: Optimizing the Construction Process, pub 2005, 4100 Executive Park Drive Cincinnati, OH

Toffler, Alvin. The Futurists, NY: Random House, 1972, ISBN 0-394-31713-0, Lib of Congress 70-39770.

Toffler, Alvin. The Eco-Spasm Report. NY: Bantam Books, Feb 1975.

Toffler, Alvin. Future Shock. NY: Bantam Books, 1970.

Toffler, Alvin. The Third Wave. NY: Bantam, 1984.

Recommended links

For those who want more information on the subject:

usa.autodesk.com/adsk/servlet/home?siteID=123112&id=129446

www10.aeccafe.com/nbc/articles/index.php?section=CorpNews&articleid=41399

www.4sitesystems.org

www.aia.org/tap_a_0903bim

www.arch-street.com/

www.blis-project.org/

www.cadence.advanstar.com/2003/0803/coverstory0803a.html

www.dbia.org

www.designatlantic.com

www.eere.energy.gov/buildings/energyplus/

www.fiatech.org

www.gdlalliance.com/

www.graphisoft.com/

www.graphisoftus.com/casestudies/Design Atlantic.pdf

www.graphisoft.com/community/success_stories/design_atlantic.html

www.nibs.org

www.onuma.com

www.sketchup.com/

www.stanford.edu/group/CIFE/

www.triglyph.org/

www.wbdg.org/design/bim.php

buildingSMART Alliance. National Institute of Building Sciences, Washington, D.C., 202-289-7800, www.iai-na.org/bsmart/.

Revit Architecture, Autodesk, Inc., San Rafael, California, 800-578-3375, usa.autodesk.com.

ArchiCad, Graphisoft U.S., Inc. Newton, Massachusetts, 617-485-4203, www.graphisoft.com/products/.

Microstation product line, Bentley Systems, Inc., Exton, Pennsylvania, 800-236-8539, www.bentley.com/en-us/products/.

Virtual Environment, IES Limited, Cambridge, MA, 617-621-1689, www.iesve.com.

Green Building Studio, Santa Rosa, CA, 707-569-7373, www.greenbuildingstudio.com.

EnergyPlus simulation software, Office of Energy Efficiency and Renewable Energy, U.S. Department of Energy, Washington, DC, 877-337-3463, www.eere.energy.gov/buildings/energyplus/.

EcoTect (and the Weather Tool and the Solar Tool), Square One, Ltd, Joondalup, Australia, 347-408-0704, www.squ1.com/products/.

Toolkit

Computers are everywhere. The Internet touches nearly everything we do. Both change so rapidly that even a focused effort cannot always keep you at the forefront. Integrated practice requires you to become an aggregator of technology. Our toolkit of software, Web sites, and processes includes the following:

Web-based project management—business—relationship—product—project—workflow management hub

Basecamp, Backpack, Campfire, Highrise—http://basecamphq. com/?referrer=designatlantic

Digital Office

Portfolio Prime Practice Management Tools—http://www.arch-street.com

Virtual Building Technology

ArchiCad—http://www.graphisoftus.com

Information and Idea Organization

MindManager Pro—http://www.mindjet.com/us

Conceptualization/sketch

ArchiCad - MSVisio—Google SketchUp

Georeferencing/mapping

Google Earth—GeoTagger—GPSPhotoLinker—Quantum GiS

Graphics

Adobe Illustrator—Adobe Photoshop—iMovie—iDVD—iPhoto—Yepp

Compositing/press

Adobe InDesign – Quark XPress - Apple Pages - Adobe Acrobat Professional

Office Applications

MSWord—MSExcel—MSVisio—MSOneNote—MSPowerPoint—Keynote - SOHO Notes

Communications

Vyew—Vonage—Skype—Campfire—freeconferencecall.com—Adium

Scheduling

MSProject - SharedPlan - Basecamp

Cost Estimating

RSMeans – D4Cost

Facilities Management

ArchiFM—Business Objects Crystal Reports

Database

FileMaker Pro – MSSQL—MySQL—OpenBase—Oracle—MSAccess

Specifications

MasterSpec

Wiki and blog

Tiddlywiki—WordPress

Trademarks and Sources

37 Signals Basecamp, Backpack, Campfire, Highrise, Portfolio Digital Practice Tools, Graphisoft ArchiCad 9 & 10, Mindjet MindManager, Google SketchUp, Google Earth—GeoTagger—GPSPhotoLinker—Quantum GiS, Adobe Illustrator—Photoshop—iMovie—iDVD—iPhoto—Yepp, Adobe InDesign—Quark Xpress—Pages, Microsoft Word—Excel—Visio – OneNote—PowerPoint—Keynote—SOHO Notes, Vyew—Vonage—Skype—Campfire – freeconferencecall.com - Adium, MSProject—SharedPlan - Basecamp, RSMeans – D4Cost – FW Dodge, ArchiFM 9—Crystal Reports - Business Objects, FileMaker Pro – MSSQL - MySQL—OpenBase—Oracle, MasterSpec, Joomla—Tiddlywiki—WordPress, Autodesk AutoCAD—Revit, Bentley

Glossary and definitions

2D—Analogous to painting or hand drafting. The architect's equivalent to word-processing. 2D computer graphics deal primarily with geometric entities (points, lines, planes, etc.). Blueprints, construction documents and anything output (or drawn on) paper are 2D.

3D—Analogous to sculpture. Prior to computers, architects manually constructed perspectives and physical (cardboard, Foamcore, balsa) models to represent a project's design concepts. Today computers have automated concept visualization. These 3D graphics can be exported to rapid prototyping systems to create physical models. 3D computer graphics rely on much of the same programming as 2D computer graphics.

3.5D—3D with the addition of limited object technology (minimal object intelligence and not integrating NCS or IFCS) or, 3D with implied movement (Ken Burns effects, trees blown by wind, moving people, etc.). This is definitely not BIM, no matter what you are told.

4D—Building Information Model with the addition of time (virtual building model with scheduling).

5D—Building Information Model with time and construction information additions (virtual building model with cost and project management).

AecXM—Architecture/Engineering/Construction-oriented Extensible Markup Language. Internet-oriented data structure for representing information used in BIM.

Agency Construction Management—Delivery process where a construction professional organization is retained to exclusively support the owner, acting in the owner's interests at every stage of the project. The owner, with the assistance of the construction manager retains separate entities for design and construction.

Beyond Information Models—Uses currently available technologies and couples them with proven business management techniques to achieve integrated practice results—today, efficiently, and economically. Beyond Information Models firms have changed their working practices, methods, and behaviors to better support their clients. They practice "small is the new big" and achieve significant practice improvements.

Building Information Model—1. To manage project information including data creation and the iterative process of exchanging data through the built environment value network: BIM includes processes by which the right information is made available to the right person at the right time. BIM adds intelligence to project data to allow data to be interpreted correctly removing attribution errors and assumptions. Or— 2. To create or work with a single archive where every item is described once: Graphical representations - drawings and non-graphical documents—specifications, schedules, and other data are included. Changes are made to any item in one place and changes flow through the system. Or—3. To represent physical and functional characteristics of an asset digitally in a reliable archive of asset information, from conception onward: without complying with the National CAD Standard and Industry Foundation Classes, it is proprietary, not interoperable and not BIM.

CAD Object—These objects are symbols and 3D representations that are static (line work with little or no intelligence). These objects are "instance-based," i.e., each use requires a new "instance" of the object, tailored to the specific situation. This approach requires a significant library of objects (i.e., one object for each size of window, another for each type of window and another for window detail). This approach results in significant storage and file size requirements to store repetitive and unconnected information.

Construction Management—Delivery practice using a construction consultant that provides design and construction advice. The owner retains design and construction services separately.

Construction Management at risk—Delivery process that delivers projects within a Guaranteed Maximum Price (GMP) in most cases. The construction manager acts as consultant to the owner in early project phases and becomes the equivalent of a general contractor during the construction phase.

Design/Bid/Build—Delivery process where an owner hold separate contracts with separate entities for design and construction. In today's environment, this is considered to be the "traditional" method for procuring design and construction services.

Design/Build—Integrated delivery process with a single source of accountability for both design and construction.

GDL—Geometric Description Language. A scriptable language for programming intelligent objects using a fraction of memory of other modeled objects. A GDL object can store 3D information (geometry, appearance, surface, material, quantity, construction, etc.), 2D information (plan representation, minimal space requirements, labels, etc.), and property information (serial numbers, price, dealer information, URL, and any other kind of database information). Multiple instances of the same object but with different appearance, material, size, etc. are kept together in one object. GDL is especially important as the Internet emerges as the best communication platform for the building industry.

Georeference—Refers to exactly locating something in the virtual world, via coordinate systems. Georeferenced buildings are tied to established coordinate systems such that they can be rapidly located in their proper place and time. Latitude, longitude, and elevation are three of the possible coordinate systems for referencing a location. Georeferencing allows for high-level studies of relationships, causes, and effects in a real-world context.

IAI—International Alliance for Interoperability. Subset of the International Standards Organization (ISO), charged with developing standards for standardizing how software represents data.

IDM—Information Delivery Manual is a document-mapping building processes, identifying results and describing actions required within process.

IFCs—Industry Foundation Classes. IFCs define how "things" such as structure, doors, walls, and fans (as well as abstract concepts such as space, organization, information exchange, and process) should be described so that different software packages can use the same information.

Integrated Practice—Uses early contribution of knowledge through utilization of new technologies, allowing architects to realize their highest potentials as designers and collaborators while expanding the value they provide throughout the project life cycle

Integration—The introduction of working practices, methods and behaviors that create a culture in which individuals and organizations are able to work together efficiently and effectively.

Intelligent Object—These Building Components can behave smart, i.e., they can adapt to changing conditions. The user can easily customize them through an interface. These objects are "rules-based," i.e., they incorporate rules that define how the object adapts to other objects, database calls, and user input parameters. Because of the "rules base," each object can represent an entire subset of an entity, i.e., one window object can represent an manufacturer's entire window line and can generate all 2D, 3D, details, finishes, shapes, and profiles. This results in significant decreases in the space required to store the equivalent information and results in very small files.

Model Server—Model servers allow centralized storage of IFC information models allowing them to be accessed and modified via the Internet. Model servers are a critical element in the long-term management of building information that will be hosted, added to, and manipulated by a large audience over a building's life cycle. The IFC-based model server is a virtual building archive, is possibly the most innovative technical approach to the future of BIM.

Multi-file approach—Multi-file systems use loosely coupled collections of drawings, each representing a portion of the complete model. These drawings are connected through various mechanisms to generate additional views of the building, reports, and schedules. Issues include the complexity of managing this loosely coupled collection of drawings and the opportunity for errors if the user manipulates the individual files outside the drawing management capabilities.

NBIMS—National BIM Standard. Standard for how information is presented via BIM, currently under development with the cooperation of the AIA, CSI, and NIBS. The National CAD Standard will become a subset of NBIMS upon completion.

NCS—National CAD Standard. Graphic standard for how information is presented via CAD systems, developed with the cooperation of the AIA, CSI, and NIBS.

NIBS—National Institute of Building Sciences. Organization supporting NCS and the IAI in the United States.

Object Oriented—A computer program may be seen as a collection of programs (objects) that act on each other. Each object can receive messages, process data, and send messages to other objects. Objects can be viewed as independent little machines or actors with a distinct role or responsibility.

Parametric—Objects that reflect real-world behaviors and attributes. A parametric model is aware of the characteristics of components and the interactions between them. It maintains consistent relationships between elements as the model is manipulated. For example, in a parametric building model, if the pitch of the roof is changed, the walls automatically follow the revised roofline.

Prototype—A working model used to test design concepts, impacts, and ideas quickly prior, to physical implementation. Integral part of a system design process created to reduce risks and costs. Can be developed incrementally so that each prototype is influenced by previous prototypes to resolve deficiencies, refine the design or increase understanding. When a prototype is developed to a level that meets project goals, it is ready for construction.

Single model approach—Revolves around a single, logical, consistent database for all information associated with the building. The building design is represented in a single virtual building that captures everything known about the asset. From this database, all project visualizations, analysis and management information can be extracted.

Value network—The Value Network adds an extra dimension to the concept of Value Chains. Value networks represent the complexity, collaboration, and interrelationships of today's organizations and environment. Value Chains are linear and Value Networks are three-dimensional.

Writeboard—Collaborative Web-based text development system that allows for editing, version control and change comparisons.

Definitions are compiled from a variety of sources including: Wikipedia, technology vendors, NIST, NBIMS, and others.

About the author

Finith E. Jernigan AIA - Born in Texas, raised in England and Germany, and now living in Maryland, the former Air Force brat builds cooperation and efficiency into every project undertaken by Design Atlantic Ltd, his Salisbury, MD firm. He lectures extensively and briefs architects, scientists, educators, technology experts, government agencies, private sector clients and Members of Congress about building information modeling and integrated processes. He has served as principal-in-charge for government and institutional projects for over twenty-five years and has personally completed more than 200 projects using virtual building models.

Finith Jernigan streamlines client decision-making and improves project visualization to achieve superior results during construction. He supports other architects and owners nationally and coaches on how to fold building information technologies into existing business operations.

He created 4SiteSystems to provide information-centric architecture, management, and planning support for institutional clients. A clear definition of expectations for each step ensures that the entire team works in concert to complete projects as effectively and efficiently as possible. The process defines working practices, methodologies, and behaviors.

Design Atlantic Ltd - is a best-practices design and planning firm founded in 1996. They have completed over 250,000 square feet of new projects, over 830,000 square feet of renovations, and planning for over 1.4 million square feet of space using

4Sitesystems processes. Design Atlantic's typical project is complex, has critical needs, and involves facilities that must remain operational throughout comprehensive renovations.

What people are saying...

BIG BIM, little bim opened my eyes to a new way of thinking about an interesting topic and the future of architectural design.

This is a great introduction to BIM and integrated practice. By using existing technologies with a new mindset, BIM can reduce inefficiency and costly mistakes in the building industry. Jernigan's models demonstrate how to reuse information, instead of recreating it every time a new system comes along. An important resource for contractors, architects, and owners.

Jernigan is at the cutting edge of BIM development with practical approaches that architects can understand and apply. I've already started implementing concepts from the book into my own architectural practice.

BIG BIM, little bim is a rare find – a book that provides thoughtful ideas on leading successful design build during a time of great changes and architectural advances. This book shows us how to manage projects and clients more effectively while also minimizing constraints in the architectural process.

Finith Jernigan's book shows how BIM allows you to leverage resources, compete in a worldwide market, and become more efficient and productive in the planning, design, construction and operation of facilities.

Owners have been the first to understand and embrace the benefits that come from an integrated process. They can easily see and understand what they get out of it. They get better projects with fewer problems.

We got a hell of a deal. "The design was perfect."

The projects have our fingerprints all over them.

We got down to the details early. The early decisions resulted in significant time and money savings.

The benefits of the process are truly amazing.

The process used for our offices gave us the opportunity for detailed input, early and often.

Having the details to make early decisions paid off. We were on track to make some expensive mistakes.

Because of the team's access to world-class specialists, we were able to analyze the City's data and determine the best location for our facilities. The architect provided detail and data to let us decide the best allocation of the money available.

What we got was huge. We got 3D renderings, a strategy and a detailed estimate that gave a good idea of the direction to go. They gave us legitimacy.

I am convinced this architect's process has allowed us to produce a far more complete report for less money and much earlier in the development process than normal.

We now understand how to achieve our dream.

The relationship gives us a "yin/yang" approach. They turn with ease and adjust quickly. Larger firms are like dinosaurs or ocean liners; they take a long time and a lot of effort to turn or change.

Being able to create a 3D model of the building was also a great asset in providing a clear vision of the project. Typically, the commissioners have to look at 2D plans and elevations and no matter how often you see those, it is hard to truly envision what you are going to get. The 3D renderings made it clear.

The flexibility of the process led to a profitable project, for us and for the owner. The design/build process worked great.

Quick Order Form

Fax orders: 443.270.6094

Telephone orders: Call 866.572.7487 toll free.

Have your credit card ready.

Email orders: fulfillment@4sitesystems.com

Postal orders: 4Site Press, 130 East Main Street, Salisbury, MD 21801-5038, USA, Telephone: 410.548.9245

Please send the following books, disks, or reports. I understand that I may return any of them for a full refund—for any reason, no questions asked.

Please send more FREE information on:

_____ Consulting _____ Speaking/Seminars _____ Mailing Lists

Name: _____

Address: _____

City: _____ State: _____ Zip: _____

Telephone: _____

Email address: _____

Credit card   VISA _____ MasterCard _____

Card number _____

Security code _____

Sales tax: Please add 5% for products shipped to Maryland addresses. Shipping by air U.S.: $8.00 for first book or disk and $5.00 for each additional product. International: $14.00 for first book or disk; $8.00 for each additional product (estimate).

Made in the USA